D0991192

MONOGRAPHS ON
STATISTICS AND APPLIED PROBABILITY

General Editors
D.R. Cox, D.V. Hinkley, D. Rubin and B.W. Silverman

The Statistical Analysis of Compositional Data
J. Aitchison

Probability, Statistics and Time
M.S. Bartlett

The Statistical Analysis of Spatial Pattern
M.S. Bartlett

Stochastic Population Models in Ecology and Epidemiology
M.S. Bartlett

Risk Theory
R.E. Beard, T. Pentikäinen and E. Pesonen

Bandit Problems – Sequential Allocation of Experiments
D.A. Berry and B. Fristedt

Transformation and Weighting in Regression
R.J. Carroll and D. Ruppert

Residuals and Influence in Regression
R.D. Cook and S. Weisberg

Point Processes
D.R. Cox and V. Isham

Analysis of Binary Data
D.R. Cox

The Statistical Analysis of Series of Events
D.R. Cox and P.A.W. Lewis

Analysis of Survival Data
D.R. Cox and D. Oakes

Queues
D.R. Cox and W.L. Smith

Stochastic Modelling and Control
M.H.A. Davis and R. Vinter

Stochastic Abundance Models
S. Engen

The Analysis of Contingency Tables
B.S. Everitt

(Full details concerning this series are available from the publishers)

Analog Estimation Methods in Econometrics

CHARLES F. MANSKI

Department of Economics
University of Wisconsin

NEW YORK   LONDON

CHAPMAN AND HALL

First published in 1988 by
Chapman and Hall
29 West 35th Street, New York, NY 10001
Published in Great Britain by
Chapman and Hall Ltd
11 New Fetter Lane, London EC4P 4EE

© *1988 Chapman and Hall* 330.18Z
  M28a

Printed in the U.S.A.

ISBN 0412 01141 7

Library of Congress Cataloging in Publication Data

Manski, Charles F.
  Analog estimation methods in econometrics/Charles F. Manski.
    p.   cm.—(Monographs on statistics and applied probability)
  Includes index.
  ISBN 0-412-01141-7
  1. Econometrics. 2. Estimation theory. I. Title. II. Series.
HB 139.M383 1988
330′.028–dc19   88-4380
                                                                  CIP

British Library Cataloguing in Publication Data

Manski, Charles F.
  Analog estimation methods in econometrics.
  —(Monographs on statistics and applied
  probability).
  1. Econometrics. Estimation
  I. Title II. Series
  330′.028

ISBN 0-412-01141-7

V8

To my parents
Samuil and Estelle J. Manski

Contents

Preface

About ten years ago I became aware of the work of Jacob Wolfowitz on minimum distance estimation of distribution functions. The minimum distance method is a simple, elegant application of the analogy principle. It seemed to me that similar ideas could be applied to the estimation of econometric models. Around 1980, my thinking gelled and I developed the approach which I called 'closest empirical distribution' (CED) estimation.

Working on CED estimation was exhilarating. For the first time, I felt that I understood the essence of the instrumental variables method introduced by Wright and Reiersol for estimation of linear models. I could now motivate Amemiya's methods for estimating nonlinear simultaneous equation models. And I realized that the analogy principle is central to statistical estimation theory.

I committed myself to writing a book on analog estimation in the spring of 1984 and began serious writing that fall. When I told my colleague Arthur Goldberger of my intentions, he excused himself and returned with his *Topics in Regression Analysis*, a book which I had not read. He pointed proudly to his statement 'the *analogy principle* of estimation... proposes that population parameters be estimated by sample statistics which have the same property in the sample as the parameters do in the population'. I subsequently decided to adopt the phrase 'analogy principle'.

I have drawn from Goldberger many good ideas and much historical perspective. Equally valuable have been frequent conceptual and technical discussions with Gary Chamberlain and Jim Powell. I have received useful comments from Chris Flinn, Jim Heckman, Whitney Newey, Ariel Pakes, and John Rust. I am also fortunate to have had Scott Thompson as a student. Scott has witnessed the evolution of this project and has proved an excellent critic. Having commented on the entire manuscript, he knows, as I do, that the book succeeds in some respects more than in others.

I am grateful to the Graduate School of The University of Wisconsin for two semester grants of release time from teaching, in 1984 and 1987. These gave me blocks of time to think and write without distraction. I am also grateful to the National Science Foundation for its support through grants SES-8319335 and SES-8605436.

Madison
November, 1987

Introduction

Estimation problems and methods

The starting point for a coherent discussion of estimation methods is a clear statement of an estimation problem. Many estimation problems have the following elements. One wants to learn some property of a specified population. It is known that the population has certain other properties. A sample of observations drawn at random from the population is available. The problem is to use the known properties of the population and the sample evidence to learn the property of interest.

Once such an estimation problem is specified, consideration of estimation methods becomes possible. The 'analogy principle' offers a means for generating estimators. The analogy principle is instantly recognized. Many authors routinely refer to sample statistics as the 'sample analogs' of corresponding population parameters. Nevertheless, the analogy principle is rarely stated explicitly. The essential idea is expressed succinctly in the following quote:

> the *analogy principle* of estimation...proposes that population parameters be estimated by sample statistics which have the same property in the sample as the parameters do in the population (Goldberger, 1968, p. 4)

This statement needs to be augmented only in that it presumes the existence of a sample statistic having the same property in the sample as the parameter does in the population. More generally, an analog estimate is one chosen so that, in some well-defined sense, the known property of the population holds as closely as possible in the sample.

Some applications

Applications of the analogy principle are ubiquitous. The sample average is an analog estimate for the population mean. Sample quantiles are analog estimates for corresponding population quantiles. The method of moments (Pearson, 1894) applies the analogy principle, as does minimum chi-square estimation (Neyman, 1949). Maximum likelihood, least squares, and least absolute deviations estimation are analog methods. Econometric contribution to the theory of analog estimation dates back to the development of instrumental variables estimation (Wright, 1928; Reiersol, 1941, 1945).

Among more recent developments, Von Mises (1947) introduced the notion of differentiable statistical functions and studied the local asymptotic behavior of their analog estimates. Wolfowitz (1953, 1957) proposed minimum distance estimation, which applies the analogy principle to the problem of estimating distribution functions. Most of the literature on robust estimation (Huber, 1981) presumes analog estimation. For example, M-estimates (Huber, 1967) are analog methods. In the recent econometric literature, Burguete, Gallant, and Souza (1982), Hansen (1982), and Manski (1983) have independently proposed analog estimation of nonlinear econometric models satisfying moment restrictions. These methods subsume the earlier instrumental variables work.

A framework for the study of estimation

The myriad applications of the analogy principle demonstrate its usefulness as a tool for generating estimators. Consideration of specific applications, however, may not convey the more general value of the analogy principle as a framework for the study of estimation.

I have found that the analogy principle offers an effective device for teaching estimation. In analog estimation, one begins by asking what one knows about the population. One then treats the sample as if it were the population. Finally, one selects an estimate that makes the known properties of the population hold as closely as possible in the sample. What could be more intuitive?

I have found that the analogy principle disciplines econometric research by focussing attention on estimation problems rather than on methods. Much of the literature proposes some new method and then looks for problems to which it can be applied. It seems more sensible to first specify an estimation problem and then seek to develop applicable estimation methods. The analogy principle forces this mode of thought. One can define an analog estimator only after one has stated the estimation problem of interest.

I have also found that analog estimation enables more realistic empirical research. The need to select from the limited menu of estimation methods that happen to appear in the literature often unduly influences the objectives, assumptions, and data of empirical research. The analogy principle allows the empirical researcher to derive an estimator that fits his problem. For each well-defined estimation problem, there generally corresponds some obvious, appropriate analog method. One can often find a multitude of useful analog methods.

I have, moreover, come to feel that the analogy principle has a certain elegance. Esthetic appeal may not suffice to make a subject worthy of study. It does help, though.

Plan of the book

This book presents elements of the theory of estimation by the analogy principle, with an emphasis on estimation problems arising in econometrics. It also offers some new contributions and calls attention to unanswered questions. Thus, the volume is both a textbook and a monograph.

The book is in three parts. Part I introduces the analogy principle and demonstrates its breadth of application. Part II presents the 'moment' problems that dominate present-day econometrics. Then Part III develops asymptotic theory for analog estimation of moment problems.

As a textbook, the volume may be found useful in the graduate econometric methods course that typically follows the student's introduction to statistics and linear models. An understanding of the concepts of asymptotic distribution theory is assumed, as is some familiarity with real analysis. At the University of Wisconsin, I have for several years based a semester course in econometric methods on this material.

As a monograph, the book offers some contributions to estimation theory. First, it proposes what seems to be a useful language for the study of analog estimation: a relevant set of concepts, a tractable system of notation, and a meaningful typology of estimation problems. Such infrastructure is essential to coherent treatment of a subject. Second, it reports results applying the analogy principle to generate consistent nonparametric estimates of density and regression functions. Hitherto, it has been thought that these nonparametric estimation problems are treatable only by non-analog methods. Third, it provides parallel treatments of consistent estimation in 'continuous' and 'step' moment problems. Whereas the theory for continuous problems has long been available, that for step problems has previously been developed only in the context of specific applications.

A disclaimer

This book makes no claim to provide a comprehensive treatment of present-day econometric methods. The scope of the book is limited in the following respects.

First, most of the asymptotic theory presented herein assumes random sampling. As an idealization, random sampling is central to statistics, much as competitive behavior is to economics. The random sampling idealization greatly simplifies the statement and proof of asymptotic theorems. Random sampling is not essential to application of the analogy principle. Brief discussions of estimation under non-random sampling processes are scattered throughout the book.

Second, the entire text assumes the perspective of classical estimation theory, to the exclusion of Bayesian analysis. The closest approach to Bayesian thinking is in Chapter 4, where prediction is posed as a decision problem under uncertainty. Even there, attention is confined to the classical problem of estimation of best predictors.

It is not clear whether the analogy principle has a Bayesian interpretation. Certainly, present-day Bayes theory does not hint at any. As matters stand, the structure of Bayes theory presumes that one faces a particular kind of estimation problem, a likelihood problem as defined in Chapters 2 and 5. This theory simply does not apply to the various non-likelihood problems treated in this book.

Third, the book rarely questions the researcher's ability to pose a well-defined, correctly specified estimation problem. To apply the analogy principle, one must state explicitly what one knows and what one wants to learn. These logically necessary requirements are undeniably burdensome in practice. It is often difficult to elicit one's information set and to make one's objectives explicit. Nevertheless, we maintain the assumption that a coherent estimation problem has been specified. And we usually assume that the asserted prior information is consistent with reality.

Finally, issues of measurability are ignored except in a few contexts where attention is warranted. The readability of a statistics book seems always to vary inversely with the rigorousness of its treatment of measurability. I want this book to be read.

Notation conventions

Theorems and lemmas are numbered within chapters and referred to by the shortest unambiguous descriptor. Consider Theorem 1 of Chapter 7. Within Chapter 7, this result is referred to as Theorem 1. In the remainder of the book, it is referred to as Theorem 7.1.

Vectors are always defined in column form, transpose notation being used for row form. Thus, if ξ is a point in K-dimensional real space, then ξ is a $K \times 1$ vector and ξ' a $1 \times K$ vector. Let $f(*)$ be a differentiable function mapping R^K into R^J. Let x index points in the domain of $f(*)$. The derivative function $\partial f(*)/\partial x'$ is a $J \times K$ matrix. This derivative evaluated at a point $\xi \in R^K$ is written $\partial f(\xi)/\partial x'$.

The 'argmin' operator is used to denote the set of argument values that minimize a function. Let $W(*)$, a function mapping a space B into the real line, be minimized on the set $B_0 \subset B$. Then $B_0 = \underset{c \in B}{\operatorname{argmin}}\, W(c)$. We shall often write equations of the form $b - \underset{c \in B}{\operatorname{argmin}}\, W(c) = 0$, where b is an element of B. Such equations are to be interpreted as saying that b is an element of the minimizing set B_0.

PART I

Estimation by the analogy principle

The vast literature on analog estimation has evolved in piecemeal fashion out of the efforts of numerous researchers to treat various classes of estimation problems. As a consequence, a standard language for study of estimation by the analogy principle has been unavailable. Moreover, some unifying ideas have gone unrecognized. Early in the writing of this book, it became clear that coherent exposition would require careful choice of terminology and the development of at least a few new concepts. Some of Part I is taken up with this task. The other objective of Part I is to survey some of the major classes of estimation problems to which the analogy principle has been applied.

Chapter 1 sets out basic concepts. We begin by posing an abstract estimation problem and by defining identification. We then introduce estimation by the analogy principle. We find that a given estimation problem generally has many alternative representations to which the analogy principle may be applied. In some problems, the derived analog estimate depends on the chosen representation. We discuss informally the consistency and efficiency of analog estimates. We also consider application of the analogy principle to data generated by non-random sampling processes.

Chapter 2 presents short case studies of five leading classes of estimation problems. These are the moment problems, nonparametric density problems, smooth statistical functions, index problems, and separable econometric models. In each case, we define the estimation problem, develop alternative representations, and derive well-known estimates by applying the analogy principle to these representations.

Chapter 3 considers the estimation of regression functions. We first define regression and call attention to some subtleties in the identification of regression functions. Following a brief discussion of 'naive' analog estimation, we describe the power and limitations of the familiar method of moments approach to the estimation of moment regressions. We then consider the problem of estimating general regression functions. This leads to a new contribution, the smallest neighborhood method for estimation of conditional probability measures.

CHAPTER 1

The analogy principle

1.1   The estimation problem

We are concerned with estimation problems of the following abstract form. A probability measure P on a measurable sample space Z characterizes a population. We know that P is an element of some space Π of probability measures on Z. We observe a sample of N independent realizations of a random variable z distributed P.

A parameter b in a specified parameter space B solves an equation

$$T(P, b) = 0 \qquad (1.1)$$

Here $T(*, *)$ is a given function mapping $\Pi \times B$ into some vector space Υ. The problem is to combine the sample data with the knowledge that $b \in B$, $P \in \Pi$, and $T(P, b) = 0$ so as to estimate b.

Unless stated otherwise, we maintain the assumption that the estimation problem is properly specified. That is, the data really are a random sample from P, the space Π does contain P, and there actually exists a $b \in B$ solving (1.1). Given that the specification is proper, we can exclude infeasible probability measures and parameter values from the spaces Π and B. A population probability measure Q is infeasible if $T(Q, c) \neq 0$ for all c in B. A parameter value c is infeasible if $T(Q, c) \neq 0$ for all Q in Π.

To introduce basic ideas it is simplest not to impose any structure beyond what has already been stated. The quantities defined here will be given content when we discuss applications. It should be understood that the abstract equation $T(P, b) = 0$ does not really restrict the relationship between P and b. For example, many of the estimation problems we shall study assert that a parameter solves some extremum problem involving P. We can express such problems by saying that b solves an equation

$$b - \operatorname*{argmin}_{c \in B} W(P, c) = 0 \qquad (1.2)$$

where $W(*, *)$ is a given function mapping $\Pi \times B$ into the real line.

1.1.1 *Identification*

In examining a specified estimation problem, one should first ask whether b could be learned if P were known. After all, knowledge of P makes sample data superfluous.

We say that b is identified relative to (P, B) if the function $T(P, *)$, defined on the domain B, takes the value zero when evaluated at b and not elsewhere. We say that the parameter is uniformly identified relative to (Π, B) if for every Q in Π there exists one c in B such that $T(Q, c) = 0$. The value c may depend on Q. In practice we can be sure that b is identified only if the parameter is uniformly identified. The reason is that we do not know P and sample data cannot reveal P with certainty.

If the parameter is uniformly identified with respect to (Π, B), then the equation $T(Q, c) = 0$ can be inverted to express c as a function of Q. That is, there exists a function $t(*)$ mapping Π onto B such that for all $(Q, c) \in \Pi \times B$,

$$T(Q, c) = 0 \Leftrightarrow c = t(Q) \tag{1.3}$$

In particular, $b = t(P)$. It is possible to think of $t(*)$ as defining the parameter as a function of the population probability measure.

1.1.2 *Identification of a function of the parameter*

It may be that b is not identified but that some interesting function of b is identified. Let $\theta(*)$ map the parameter space B into a space Θ. If $\theta(*)$ is one-to-one, then $\theta(b)$ is identified if and only if b is. On the other hand, if $\theta(*)$ is many-to-one, then $\theta(b)$ may be identified even though b is not. To be precise, $\theta(b)$ is identified if $\theta(c) = \theta(b)$ for all c in B such that $T(P, c) = 0$.

1.2 Analog estimates

Let P_N be the empirical measure of the sample of N draws from P. That is, P_N is the multinomial probability distribution that places probability $1/N$ on each of the N observations of z. The analogy principle suggests that to estimate b one should substitute the function $T(P_N, *)$ for $T(P, *)$ and use

$$B_N \equiv [c \in B: T(P_N, c) = 0] \tag{1.4}$$

Equation (1.4) defines analog estimation for problems where P_N is an element of Π. In such problems $T(P_N, *)$ is well defined and has at least one zero in B. So B_N is the (set-valued) analog estimate of b.

Equation (1.4) does not explain how to apply the analogy principle to problems in which the empirical measure and the population measure are known to differ. We have so far defined $T(*, *)$ only on the space $\Pi \times B$ of feasible population distributions and parameter values. The function $T(P_N, *)$ is as yet undefined for P_N not in Π.

Let Φ denote the space of all multinomial distributions on Z. To define $T(P_N, *)$ for every sample size and all sample realizations, it suffices to extend $T(*, *)$ from $\Pi \times B$ to the domain $(\Pi \cup \Phi) \times B$. Two very different approaches prove useful.

1.2.1 Mapping P_N into Π

One approach is to map P_N into Π. Select a function $\pi(*)$ with domain $\Pi \cup \Phi$ and range Π which maps every feasible population distribution into itself. That is, let $\pi(*)$ be any function such that $Q \in \Pi \cup \Phi \Rightarrow \pi(Q) \in \Pi$ and $Q \in \Pi \Rightarrow \pi(Q) = Q$. Now replace the equation $T(P, b) = 0$ with

$$T[\pi(P), b] = 0 \tag{1.5}$$

This substitution leaves the estimation problem unchanged as $T[\pi(Q), *] = T(Q, *)$ for all $Q \in \Pi$. Moreover, $\pi(P_N) \in \Pi$; so $T[\pi(P_N), *]$ is defined and has a zero in B. The analogy principle applied to (1.5) yields

$$B_{N\pi} \equiv [c \in B: T\{\pi(P_N), c\} = 0] \tag{1.6}$$

When P_N is in Π, this analog estimate is the same as the one defined in (1.4). When P_N is not in Π, the estimate (1.6) depends on the selected function $\pi(*)$; hence we write $B_{N\pi}$ rather than B_N.

Two applications of the mapping approach will be presented later. One is to nonparametric estimation of density functions; see Section 2.2. The other is to nonparametric estimation of regression functions; see Chapter 3.

1.2.2 *Direct extension*

Sometimes there is a natural direct way to extend $T(*, *)$. A leading example is the class of moment equations. These are estimation problems in which

$$T(Q, c) = \int g(z, c) \, dQ \tag{1.7}$$

for $(Q, c) \in \Pi \times B$. Here $g(*, c)$ is a given measurable function on Z. When $T(*, *)$ has this form, it is natural to let

$$T(P_N, c) = \int g(z, c) \, dP_N \tag{1.8}$$

Assume now that $T(P_N, *)$ has been defined directly. Whenever $T(P_N, *)$ has a zero in B, (1.4) gives the analog estimate. If P_N is not in Π, however, it may be that $T(P_N, c) \neq 0$ for all c in B. Then the analogy principle suggests selection of an estimate that makes $T(P_N, *)$ as close as possible to zero in some sense.

To put this idea into practice, select an origin-preserving function $r(*)$ which maps values of $T(*, *)$ into the non-negative real half-line. That is, let $r(*)$ be any function from Υ into $[0, \infty)$ such that $T = 0 \Leftrightarrow r(T) = 0$. For example, if Υ is a normed space, setting $r(T) \equiv \| T \|$ will do.

Now replace the equation $T(P, b) = 0$ with

$$r[T(P, b)] = 0 \tag{1.9}$$

This substitution leaves the estimation problem unchanged as $T(Q, c) = 0 \Leftrightarrow r[T(Q, c)] = 0$ for all $(Q, c) \in \Pi \times B$. To estimate b, minimize on B the sample analog of $r[T(P, *)]$. Provided only that $r[T(P_N, *)]$ attains its minimum on B, the analog estimate is

$$B_{Nr} \equiv \underset{c \in B}{\operatorname{argmin}} \, r[T(P_N, c)] \tag{1.10}$$

When P_N is in Π, this estimate is the same as the one defined in (1.4). When P_N is not in Π, $T(P_N, *)$ may nonetheless have a zero in B; if so, the estimate remains as in (1.4). If $T(P_N, *)$ is everywhere non-zero, the estimate (1.10) depends on the selected function $r(*)$; hence we write B_{Nr} rather than B_N.

1.2.3 *Alternative representations of estimation problems*

In deriving the analog estimates $B_{N\pi}$ and B_{Nr}, we observed that the equations $T(P, b) = 0$, $T[\pi(P), b] = 0$, and $r[T(P, b)] = 0$ express the same knowledge relating P to b. This fact illustrates a general point: a given estimation problem may have many alternative representations.

When P_N is in Π, representation has no consequence for estimation by the analogy principle. Whatever representation one chooses, the analog estimate for b is B_N. When P_N is not in Π, alternative representations typically yield distinct analog estimates. Recall that the estimates $B_{N\pi}$ and B_{Nr} vary with the function $\pi(*)$ or $r(*)$ that one selects.

The representations introduced thus far do not exhaust the possibilities. As we study specific estimation problems, we shall note some useful generalizations. We shall not, however, seek to develop an exhaustive typology of representations.

1.2.4 *Cardinality of analog estimates*

The literature on estimation focusses attention on point estimates of parameters. We, on the other hand, have defined an analog estimate to be the set of parameter values that solve the sample analog of a population problem. In many applications, analog estimates are singletons. Where an estimate contains more than one element, one may wish to extract a point estimate by applying some auxiliary selection rule. We shall usually not do so. The analogy principle gives no reason to isolate one point for special attention.

1.2.5 *Estimation of a function of the parameter*

An analog estimate of a function of b is obtained by evaluating the function at an estimate of b. Let $\theta(*)$ mapping B into Θ be the function of interest. When P_N is in Π, then $\Theta_N \equiv [\theta(c), c \in B_N]$ is the estimate of $\theta(b)$. When P_N is not in Π, estimates $\Theta_{N\pi}$ and Θ_{Nr} may be obtained by applying $\theta(*)$ to $B_{N\pi}$ and B_{Nr}.

1.3 Consistency and efficiency of analog estimates

1.3.1 *Consistency*

We have said that in examining an estimation problem, one should first ask whether the parameter of interest is identified. Assume that identification has been shown and that one now contemplates estimation. In evaluating a proposed estimation method, one should first ask whether the method is consistent. That is, does the method yield estimates that in some sense converge to the parameter as sample data accumulates?

Analog estimates are consistent under quite general conditions. The fundamental theorems that make this so are referred to generically as laws of large numbers. These theorems show that the empirical measure P_N converges in various senses to the population measure P. Of course laws of large numbers do not *per se* imply consistency. The chosen representation of the estimation problem must be appropriately smooth. A heuristic explanation follows.

Consider an estimation problem where all possible realizations of P_N are in Π. Provided that the function $T(P_N, *)$ varies smoothly with P_N, the laws of large numbers imply that $T(P_N, *)$ tends to behave increasingly like $T(P, *)$ as $N \to \infty$. In particular, the zeros on B of $T(P_N, *)$ tend to occur increasingly near the zeros of $T(P, *)$. Given identification, $T(P, *)$ is zerod at b alone. So the analog estimate B_N converges to b.

Now consider a problem where not all realizations of P_N are in Π. Select a function $\pi(*)$ and estimate b by $B_{N\pi}$ defined in (1.6). Then we are concerned with the behavior of $T[\pi(P_N), *]$ as $N \to \infty$. Provided that $\pi(P_N)$ varies smoothly with P_N, the argument of the preceding paragraph implies that the estimate $B_{N\pi}$ converges to b.

Alternatively, select a function $r(*)$ and estimate b by B_{Nr} defined in (1.10). Then we are concerned with the behavior of $r[T(P_N, *)]$ as $N \to \infty$. Provided that $r[T(P_N, *)]$ varies smoothly with P_N, the minima on B of $r[T(P_N, *)]$ tend to occur increasingly near the minima of $r[T(P, *)]$. Given identification, $r[T(P, *)]$ is minimized at b alone. So the estimate B_{Nr} converges to b.

Rigorous demonstrations of consistency require that one specify the desired sense of convergence of the estimate to b and give content to the above provisos that $T(P_N, *)$, $\pi(P_N)$, and $r[T(P_N, *)]$ vary smoothly with P_N. It would be too much to expect one consistency theorem to cover all the applications of interest. To the contrary, the literature reports a multitude of consistency results covering various classes of estimation problems.

We shall later give proofs of consistency for analog estimation of two classes of estimation problems. A result reported in Chapter 3 proves pointwise weak consistency for an analog estimate of nonparametric regressions. A group of theorems developed in Chapter 7 prove strong consistency for method of moments estimates of parameters in finite-dimensional moment problems.

One would like to know whether there exist identified estimation problems for which there are no consistent analog estimators but there are consistent non-analog estimators. (A non-analog estimator is one that cannot be obtained by applying the analogy principle to some representation of the estimation problem.) As it stands, I have no example of such a problem.

1.3.2 *Efficiency*

Given an estimation problem for which there exist consistent analog estimates, it is natural to ask whether there is an efficient such estimate, some notion of efficient estimation having been specified. The following comments are speculative but may be helpful.

One should not expect that there always is an efficient analog estimate. After all, the analogy principle disregards two kinds of information that may be relevant to estimation. First, it uses the sample data only through the empirical measure, which does not preserve information about the sample size. Second, it uses the empirical measure only to replace P in the function $T(P, *)$. That is, the analogy principle ignores restrictions on P that are not expressed by the equation $T(P, b) = 0$.

To fully understand the efficiency properties of analog estimation, it may be necessary to embed the problem of estimating b within the larger problem of estimating the pair (P, b). First one would consider the question of efficient estimation of (P, b). Then one would seek to determine the circumstances in which using P_N to estimate P suffices to obtain an efficient estimate of b.

It seems reasonable to think that the analogy principle makes efficient use of the available information whenever the empirical measure is in Π. When P_N is in Π, the hypothesis $(P, b) = (P_N, B_N)$ is compatible with the available information. Given this, it is difficult to imagine that one can do better than use (P_N, B_N) to estimate (P, b).

The efficiency of analog estimation seems more questionable in those cases where P_N is not in Π. Here a multitude of analog estimates may exist, each derived from a different representation of the estimation problem. The hypothesis $P_N = P$ is not compatible with the available information. This suggests that one can improve on any estimator of b that uses P_N as an estimate for P.

Although suggestive, the reasoning of the last paragraph does not imply that analog estimation is necessarily inefficient when P_N is not in Π. To the contrary, it is known that when efficiency is defined in local asymptotic terms, efficient analog estimates often exist. A cornerstone of classical statistics is the finding that the maximum likelihood method is asymptotically efficient for estimation of a population density function known to be a member of a smooth finite-dimensional family of densities. And recent research proves the existence of efficient method of moments estimates of parameters in smooth moment problems. These results will be presented in Chapters 8 and 9.

1.3.3 Non-random sampling

In posing the abstract estimation problem of Section 1.1, we assumed that the sample data are drawn independently from one population. It is important to understand that random sampling is no more than a useful simplifying idealization; it is not essential to the success of analog estimation. The analogy principle works whenever the sampling process is such that relevant features of the empirical measure converge to corresponding population features. Three leading examples follow.

First consider stationary time series problems. Here the data are observations at N dates from a single realization of a stationary stochastic process whose marginal distribution is P. So we do not have a random sample from P. Nevertheless, dependent sampling versions of the laws of large numbers show that P_N converges to P in various senses as $N \to \infty$.

Next consider independent sampling from a sequence of populations. Here the estimation problem assumes that a sequence of probability measures P^i, $i = 1, \ldots, \infty$ characterize the sequence of populations. The data are independent realizations of random variables $z^i, i = 1, \ldots, N$, where z^i is distributed P^i.

Independent sampling problems assume that the measures $\{P^i\}$ share some common feature. Perhaps they have the same mean or a common regression function. Let $f(*)$ denote the common feature; that is, $f(*)$ is a function on the space of probability measures on Z with $f(P^1) = f(P^i), i = 1, \ldots, \infty$. The parameter b is known to solve an equation

$$T[f(P^1), b] = 0 \qquad (1.11)$$

Subject to smoothness conditions, the analogy principle works provided that $f(P_N)$ converges to $f(P^1)$ as $N \to \infty$. Independent sampling versions of the laws of large numbers give conditions implying such convergence.

A third example is stratified random sampling. Let the sample space Z be partitioned into a finite set of mutually exclusive and exhaustive subspaces (strata) $Z_s, s = 1, \ldots, S$. For each s, let $P|s$ be the population measure conditional on the event $[z \in Z_s]$. These conditional measures are related to the population measure P by the equation

$$P = \sum_s P(Z_s) P|s \qquad (1.12)$$

where $P(Z_s)$ is the marginal probability of membership in stratum s.

For each s, let N_s observations be drawn at random from $P|s$. Let $P|s_{N_s}$ denote the resulting empirical measure. Define the stratum-weighted empirical measure

$$Q_N \equiv \sum_s P(Z_s) P|s_{N_s} \qquad (1.13)$$

Provided that the stratum marginals $P(Z_s)$ are known, Q_N is computable. Provided that $N_s \to \infty$ for all s, Q_N converges to P. Given these two conditions, Q_N is a usable sample analog for P.

CHAPTER 2

Varieties of estimation problems

Five classes of estimation problems are described here. Each class is defined by the structure it places on the equation $T(P, b) = 0$ relating the parameter to the population. Each is special enough and important enough to have spawned a distinct literature.

These five classes of estimation problems are not mutually exclusive. Many familiar problems are in the intersection of several classes. Such problems may be treated from the perspectives of various branches of estimation theory.

2.1 Moment problems

Much of present-day econometrics is concerned with estimation of the parameter b solving an extremum problem

$$b - \underset{c \in B}{\operatorname{argmin}} \int h(z, c) \, dP = 0 \qquad (2.1)$$

where $h(*, *)$ is a given function mapping $Z \times B$ into the real line. The space Π includes only probability measures Q for which the integrals $\int h(z, c) \, dQ, c \in B$ exist. Another important part of econometric work is concerned with estimation of the parameter b solving an equation

$$\int g(z, b) \, dP = 0 \qquad (2.2)$$

Here $g(*, *)$ is a given function mapping $Z \times B$ into a real vector space. Again Π includes only measures Q for which $\int g(z, c) \, dQ, c \in B$ exist.

When the empirical measure P_N is in Π, application of the analogy principle to (2.1) yields the estimate

$$B_N = \underset{c \in B}{\operatorname{argmin}} \int h(z, c) \, dP_N \qquad (2.3)$$

The analogy principle applied to (2.2) yields

$$B_N = \left[c \in B: \int g(z, c)\, dP_N = 0 \right] \qquad (2.4)$$

When P_N is not in Π, one might either map P_N into Π or extend the domain of $T(*, *)$ directly. The latter approach is simplest; the natural sample analogs of the expected values of the functions $h(z, *)$ and $g(z, *)$ are the sample averages $\int h(z, *)\, dP_N$ and $\int g(z, *)\, dP_N$. So (2.3) and (2.4) remain analog estimates of the parameters solving (2.1) and (2.2).

It remains only to consider the possibility that the estimate (2.3) or (2.4) is empty. In applications, $\int h(z, *)\, dP_N$ generally has a minimum. On the other hand, $\int g(z, *)\, dP_N$ often has no zero. In that case, one may select an origin-preserving transformation $r(*)$ and replace (2.2) with $r[\int g(z, b)\, dP] = 0$, as in (1.9). Minimizing the sample analog yields the estimate

$$B_{Nr} \equiv \operatorname*{argmin}_{c \in B} r \left[\int g(z, c)\, dP_N \right] \qquad (2.5)$$

Estimation problems relating b to P by (2.1) or (2.2) will be called moment problems. Use of the term 'moment' rather than the equally descriptive 'expectation', 'mean', or 'integral' honors the early work of K. Pearson on the 'method of moments'.

2.1.1 The method of moments

Pearson (1894) studied the special case of (2.2) in which $g(*, *)$ has the separable form

$$g(z, b) = \gamma(b) - y(z) \qquad (2.6)$$

Here the parameter space B is a subset of K-dimensional real space, $\gamma(*)$ is a given function mapping B into R^K, and $y(*)$ is a given function mapping Z into R^K. Thus b solves the equation

$$\gamma(b) - \int y(z)\, dP = 0 \qquad (2.7)$$

Let Y denote the convex hull of $[y(\zeta), \zeta \in Z]$. Assume that $\gamma(*)$ maps B one-to-one and onto Y. Given that $y(*)$ is integrable, the mean value $\int y(z)\, dP$ exists and is in Y; hence the parameter is uniformly identified. In particular,

$$b = \gamma^{-1}\left(\int y(z)\,dP \right) \tag{2.8}$$

The sample average $\int y(z)\,dP_N$ is also an element of Y. So application of the analogy principle yields the point estimate

$$b_N \equiv \gamma^{-1}\left[\int y(z)\,dP_N \right] \tag{2.9}$$

This is the method of moments estimate for b.

In the statistical literature, the method of moments is invariably described as a sometimes simple but often inefficient approach to estimation. Chronicling his late father's research, E. S. Pearson (1936, pp. 219–20) says of K. Pearson (1894):

> The paper is particularly noteworthy for its introduction of the method of moments as a means of fitting a theoretical curve to observational data. This method is not claimed to be the best, but is advocated from the utilitarian standpoint on the grounds that it appears to give excellent fits and provides algebraic solutions for calculating the constants of the curve which are analytically possible.

In his landmark text, Cramer (1946, p. 498) states:

> Under general conditions, the method of moments will thus yield estimates such that the asymptotic efficiency...exists. As pointed out by R.A. Fisher..., this quantity is, however, often considerably less than 1, which implies that the estimates given by the method of moments are not the 'best' possible from the efficiency point of view, i.e. they do not have the smallest possible variance in large samples. Nevertheless, on account of its practical expediency the method will often render good service.

This assessment continues to prevail. In fact, with computation decreasingly a concern in applied work, recent statistics texts tend to treat the method of moments cursorily, if at all.

The conclusion that the method of moments is inefficient rests on the unstated premise that the probability measure P is a member of a family of measures indexed by the elements of B. Let $[\tau(c), c \in B]$ be a family of distinct probability measures on Z and let $\Pi = [\tau(c), c \in B]$.

That is, assume it known that $P = \tau(b)$ for some b in B. Now select any function $\gamma(*)$ and define

$$\gamma(*) \equiv \int y(z)\,\mathrm{d}\tau(*) \tag{2.10}$$

as a function on B. Then (2.10) implies a moment equation of the form (2.7). Provided that $\gamma(*)$ is well-behaved, the resulting method of moments estimate for b is consistent and asymptotically normal.

Not surprisingly, the estimate based on one given choice of $y(*)$ often has asymptotic variance that exceeds the best that can be attained given the knowledge that P is in $[\tau(c), c \in B]$. The heuristic reason is that restriction of P to the finite-dimensional family of distributions $[\tau(c), c \in B]$ implies infinitely many moment restrictions relating P to b. Any particular method of moments estimator utilizes only K of these restrictions. So method of moments estimation does not use all of the information presumed to be available.

It should be recognized that criticism of the method of moments for using only a subset of the available information carries with it an implicit recommendation: the method of moments retains useful properties when the available information is, in fact, limited. The probability measure P need not be in $[\tau(c), c \in B]$. All that is required is that b solve (2.7). The ability to proceed with estimations based on this limited knowledge is valuable when a researcher questions the validity of stronger restrictions.

2.1.2 Varieties of moment problems

One hundred years after the introduction of the method of moments, we find a vast literature on analog estimation of moment problems. This book explores various major branches of this literature. Moment regressions are introduced in Chapter 3. Prediction problems are studied in Chapter 4. Likelihood problems are examined in Section 2.4, in Chapter 5, and in Section 8.4. Moment problems implied by econometric models are introduced in Section 2.5 and then studied in depth in Chapter 6.

These varieties of moment problems encompass an astonishing range of specifications. The population probability measure may be known to be among a small set of feasible measures or may be entirely unrestricted. The parameter of interest may be a best predictor function or a construct of economic theory.

What unifies the class of moment problems is a common formal structure that makes available a common asymptotic estimation theory. Chapters 7 and 8 develop this estimation theory for the subclass of finite-dimensional moment problems. The qualifier 'finite-dimensional' describes those problems in which the parameter space B is a finite-dimensional real space and, in the case of moment equations, in which the range space of $g(*, *)$ is finite dimensional. Sections 9.1 and 9.2 discuss the theory available for more general moment problems.

2.2 Nonparametric density problems

Nonparametric density estimation is a problem which might seem to defy treatment by the analogy principle. To set up the problem, let Z be K-dimensional real space. Let Π be the set of all probability measures on R^K that are absolutely continuous with respect to Lebesgue measure, denoted μ. For Q in Π, let $\varphi_\mu(*, Q)$ denote the density function of Q with respect to μ. Thus, $\varphi_\mu(*, Q)$ maps R^K into $[0, \infty)$ and

$$Q(A) = \int_A \varphi_\mu(z, Q) \, d\mu \qquad (2.11)$$

for every measurable subset A of R^K. Let the parameter space B be the space of all functions mapping R^K into $[0, \infty)$ whose Lebesgue integral equals one. The true parameter b is the function solving the equation

$$b(*) - \varphi_\mu(*, P) = 0 \qquad (2.12)$$

Being multinomial, the empirical measure is not absolutely continuous with respect to Lebesgue measure. So P_N is not in Π. To apply the analogy principle, we may either map P_N into Π or somehow extend the definition of a Lebesgue density to multinomial distributions. We shall choose the first approach. In particular, we shall use the analogy principle to derive a version of the kernel estimation method developed by Rosenblatt (1956) and Parzen (1962).

To map P_N into Π, select a function $\sigma(*)$ that maps $\Pi \cup \Phi$ into $[0, \infty)$ and satisfies the condition $\sigma(Q) = 0 \Leftrightarrow Q \in \Pi$. Thus, $\sigma(*)$ distinguishes measures that are absolutely continuous from ones that are not. Select an absolutely continuous measure G and let δ be a random variable distributed G. Given any probability measure Q on R^K, let $z(Q)$ denote a random variable distributed Q, with $z(Q)$ independent of δ. Let $Q \oplus \sigma(Q)G$ denote the probability measure of the random variable $z(Q) + \sigma(Q)\delta$. Now define

$$\pi(Q) \equiv Q \oplus \sigma(Q)G \tag{2.13}$$

and replace (2.12) with

$$b(*) - \varphi_\mu[*, \pi(P)] = 0 \tag{2.14}$$

This substitution leaves the estimation problem unchanged. Simply observe that for Q in Π, $\sigma(Q) = 0$. Hence, $\pi(Q) = Q$. So (2.12) and (2.14) both state that b is the density of P.

Moreover, $\pi(Q)$ is absolutely continuous even when Q is not. To see this, let $g(*)$ denote the density of G. Let $F(*, Q)$ denote the distribution function of the random variable $z(Q) + \sigma(Q)\delta$. When Q is not in Π, $\sigma(Q) > 0$. Hence, evaluated at any ζ in R^K,

$$F(\zeta, Q) \equiv \text{Prob}\,[z(Q) + \sigma(Q)\delta \leqq \zeta] = \int\!\!\int_{-\infty}^{[\zeta - z(Q)]/\sigma(Q)} g(\delta)\,d\delta\,dQ \tag{2.15}$$

This distribution function is differentiable. In particular,

$$\partial^K F(\zeta, Q)/\partial \zeta_1 \ldots \partial \zeta_K = 1/\sigma(Q)^K \int g[\{\zeta - z(Q)\}/\sigma(Q)]\,dQ \tag{2.16}$$

Differentiability of a distribution function implies absolute continuity of the underlying probability measure. The density equals the derivative (2.16). So the density of $\pi(Q)$ at ζ is

$$\varphi_\mu[\zeta, \pi(Q)] = 1/\sigma(Q)^K \int g[\{\zeta - z(Q)\}/\sigma(Q)]\,dQ \tag{2.17}$$

The above shows that the probability measure $Q \oplus \sigma(Q)G$ is a smoothed version of Q. So $\pi(*)$ defined in (2.13) maps $\Pi \cup \Phi$ into Π in the manner specified in Section 1.2. Applying the analogy principle to (2.14), we now obtain as the estimated density at ζ

$$b_N(\zeta) \equiv 1/\sigma(P_N)^K \int g[\{\zeta - z(P_N)\}/\sigma(P_N)]\,dP_N$$

$$= 1/\sigma(P_N)^K \frac{1}{N} \sum_{i=1}^{N} g[(\zeta - z_i)/\sigma(P_N)] \tag{2.18}$$

where $z_i, i = 1, \ldots, N$ are the sample realizations of z. Estimates of the form (2.18) are called kernel estimates. The density $g(*)$ chosen by the researcher is the kernel. $\sigma(*)$ is referred to as the smoothing function.

In the literature on density estimation, the kernel method has not been thought of as an application of the analogy principle. To the contrary, the convention has been to think of $\sigma(*)$ as a function of the sample size, not as one defined on the space of probability measures. If our analogy principle version of kernel estimation is to be useful, we need to provide guidance on the specification of $\sigma(*)$ as a function on $\Pi \cup \Phi$.

Heuristically, we would like $\sigma(Q)$ to be closer to zero, the less Q deviates from an absolutely continuous measure. Given that the elements of $\Pi \cup \Phi$ are measures with no singular continuous component, absolute continuity of an element of $\Pi \cup \Phi$ is equivalent to continuity. So we would like $\sigma(Q)$ to be closer to zero, the less Q deviates from a continuous measure.

Perhaps the simplest reasonable index of a probability measure's deviation from continuity is the maximum of its point masses. Thus, define

$$M(Q) \equiv \max_{\zeta \in R^1} Q(\zeta) \qquad (2.19)$$

and set

$$\sigma(Q) = s[M(Q)] \qquad (2.20)$$

where $s(*)$ is some strictly increasing function mapping $[0, 1]$ into $[0, \infty)$ and satisfying the condition $s(0) = 0$.

Continuity of the population measure P implies that with probability one, no realization of z occurs in the sample more than once; so all of the point masses of the empirical measure equal $1/N$. Hence,

$$\sigma(P_N) = s(1/N) \qquad (2.21)$$

with probability one. This effectively translates $\sigma(*)$ into a smoothing function which varies with sample size. We can therefore apply available results (see Prakasa Rao, 1983; or Silverman, 1986) to determine the conditions under which the estimate (2.18) is consistent. It turns out that the kernel estimate is consistent if and only if the chosen function $s(*)$ satisfies the additional condition $Ns(1/N)^K \to \infty$ as $N \to \infty$. Note that this result places no restrictions on the chosen kernel density $g(*)$.

2.3 Smooth statistical functions

In Chapter 1, we noted that when b is uniformly identified, one can think of the parameter as a function of the population probability measure. That is, there is a $t(*)$ mapping Π onto B such that

$$b - t(P) = 0 \qquad\qquad (2.22)$$

Following Von Mises (1947), we refer to $t(*)$ as a 'statistical function'.

When P_N is in Π, the analog estimate of $t(P)$ is $t(P_N)$. When P_N is not in Π, let the domain of $t(*)$ somehow be extended to the space $\Pi \cup \Phi$. Then we may continue to say that $t(P_N)$ is the analog estimate.

Representation of an estimation problem by (2.22) and estimation of b by $t(P_N)$ is particularly appealing when the statistical function $t(*)$ varies smoothly in a neighborhood of P. Smoothness of $t(*)$ makes it easy to analyze the asymptotic behavior of $t(P_N)$. Moreover, smoothness brings with it the desirable property of 'robustness'.

2.3.1 *Smoothness and asymptotic analysis*

When $t(*)$ is appropriately smooth, characterization of the asymptotic behavior of $t(P_N)$ is almost trivial. Perhaps the most striking demonstration of this is proof of consistency by the well-known 'continuous mapping' theorem.

Theorem 1
Let $t(*)$ be a given statistical function. Let λ be a given metric on B. Assume that there exists some metric ρ on $\Pi \cup \Phi$ such that:

 (i) P_N converges to P almost surely (or in probability) with respect to ρ.
(ii) $t(*)$ is continuous at P with respect to the topologies generated by ρ and λ.

Then $t(P_N)$ converges to $t(P)$ with respect to λ almost surely (or in probability).   ∎

PROOF Let $\varepsilon > 0$. Continuity of $t(*)$ implies that for every $\varepsilon > 0$ there exists a $\delta > 0$ such that $\rho(Q, P) < \delta \Rightarrow \lambda[t(Q), t(P)] < \varepsilon$.

Suppose that $P_N \to P$ with respect to ρ almost surely. Then for almost every sample sequence, there exists a finite sample size N_0 (which may depend on the sample sequence and on ε) such that $\rho(P_N, P) < \delta$ for $N > N_0$. Hence, for almost every sample sequence, $\lambda[t(P_N), t(P)] < \varepsilon$ eventually.

Suppose that $P_N \to P$ with respect to ρ in probability. Continuity of $t(*)$ implies that $\text{Prob}\,[\lambda\{t(P_N), t(P)\} < \varepsilon] \geqslant \text{Prob}\,[\rho(P_N, P) < \delta]$. But $\text{Prob}\,[\rho(P_N, P) < \delta] \to 1$ as $N \to \infty$. Hence $\text{Prob}\,[\lambda\{t(P_N), t(P)\} < \varepsilon] \to 1$.   Q.E.D.

Whereas continuity of $t(*)$ simplifies proof of consistency, differentiability eases derivation of limiting distributions. This topic will not be pursued here. For a discussion, see Serfling (1980, Chapter 6).

2.3.2 Smoothness and robustness

A statistical function that varies smoothly is also said to be robust. Use of the term 'robust' as a synonym for 'smooth' is motivated readily by consideration of a contaminated sampling problem studied by Huber (1981).

Suppose that one wishes to learn $t(P)$ but P_N is not obtained by random sampling from P. Most observations are drawn from P but a few are drawn from another probability measure Q. One does not know which observations are proper and which are contaminated. In this setting, $t(P_N)$ will generally not converge to $t(P)$. Nevertheless, it is still desirable that $t(P_N)$ converge to a point close to $t(P)$. This will be the case if $t(*)$ is appropriately smooth at P and if the frequency of contamination is sufficiently small. So analog estimates of smooth statistical functions are robust against (that is, insensitive to) occasional contamination in the sampling process.

2.3.3 Smooth statistical function theory and econometrics

The above brief discussion should suffice to indicate the power of the theory that is available for examining the properties of analog estimates of smooth statistical functions. To date, this theory has been applied very fruitfully to the problem of estimating location parameters for probability measures on the real line. On the other hand, there have been only a few applications to the kinds of estimation problems faced in econometrics. One would like to know why.

A partial explanation is that in econometric estimation problems it is often difficult to determine the smoothness properties of the statistical function defining the parameter of interest. In moment extremum problems, $t(*)$ is an argmin operator. In nonlinear moment equations, $t(*)$ is defined implicitly. It is not easy to determine in what senses such statistical functions are and are not smooth.

2.4   Index problems

The parameter space B is said to index the space Π of probability measures if there is a known function $\tau(*)$ that maps B onto Π. Thus, $\Pi = [\tau(c), c \in B]$ and b solves the equation

$$P - \tau(b) = 0 \qquad (2.23)$$

When P_N is in Π, the analog estimate for b is

$$B_N \equiv [c \in B : P_N = \tau(c)] \qquad (2.24)$$

When P_N is not in Π, the literature offers a number of approaches to estimation of b. These are obtained by applying the analogy principle to alternative representations of the estimation problem. In Section 2.1, we noted that index problems imply moment equations relating b to P; so the method of moments is one approach. Here we call attention to two others.

2.4.1 *Minimum distance estimation*

Select a metric ρ on the space $\Pi \cup \Phi$ and replace (2.23) with

$$\rho[P, \tau(b)] = 0 \qquad (2.25)$$

This substitution, which says that the distance between P and $\tau(b)$ is zero, leaves the estimation problem unchanged. The analogy principle now suggests that to estimate b, one might minimize the distance between P_N and $\tau(*)$ in the sense of ρ. The result is the 'minimum distance' estimate

$$B_{N\rho} \equiv \operatorname*{argmin}_{c \in B} \rho[P_N, \tau(c)] \qquad (2.26)$$

introduced by Wolfowitz (1953, 1957).

Minimum distance estimation is a class of analog estimation methods whose members are distinguished by the chosen metric ρ. Following the original work of Wolfowitz, it has been observed that the theme of minimum distance estimation does not require that ρ be a metric. In particular, (2.25) remains a valid representation of the index problem if ρ is any function mapping $(\Pi \cup \Phi) \times \Pi$ into $[0, \infty)$ such that $\rho(Q_1, Q_2) = 0$ if and only if $Q_1 = Q_2$. Analog estimates obtained using such general ρ are termed 'minimum discrepancy' estimates. See Sahler (1970).

2.4.2 *The maximum likelihood method*

Assume that all the probability measures in Π are absolutely continuous with respect to a common measure v on Z. For Q in Π, let $\varphi_v(*, Q)$ denote the density of Q with respect to v. Now replace (2.23) with

$$\varphi_v(*, P) - \varphi_v[*, \tau(b)] = 0 \qquad (2.27)$$

This substitution, which says that the density of P equals that of $\tau(b)$, leaves the estimation problem unchanged.

Now assume that the expectation of $\log \varphi_v[z, \tau(c)]$ with respect to P exists for each c in B. Then b solves (2.27) if and only if b also solves the 'likelihood' problem

$$b - \underset{c \in B}{\operatorname{argmax}} \int \log \varphi_v[z, \tau(c)] \, \mathrm{d}P = 0 \qquad (2.28)$$

A version of this well-known result is proved in Chapter 5. See also Rao (1973, p. 58). Applying the analogy principle to this moment extremum problem yields the maximum likelihood estimate

$$B_N \equiv \underset{c \in B}{\operatorname{argmax}} \int \log \varphi_v[z, \tau(c)] \, \mathrm{d}P_N \qquad (2.29)$$

first studied by Fisher (1925).

It is of interest to compare the minimum distance and maximum likelihood approaches to the estimation of index problems. Maximum likelihood is favored for its asymptotic efficiency properties and for the relative simplicity of its moment extremum form. Minimum distance has a larger domain of application; the measures in Π need not be absolutely continuous with respect to any common measure. Some recent literature has emphasized the superior robustness of certain minimum distance estimates. See Parr and Schucany (1980).

2.5 Separable econometric models

The reader may have noted that we have yet made no mention of unobservable random variables. The abstract equation $T(P, b) = 0$ relates a parameter to a probability measure generating realizations of an observable random variable.

Econometric models, on the other hand, typically posit restrictions relating the realizations of observable and unobservable random variables. Suppose that one wishes to estimate a parameter of the process generating these realizations. Analog estimation methods may be applied if one is able to use the available information to formulate an estimation problem relating the parameter of interest to observables.

2.5.1 The estimation problem

To fix ideas, consider the following abstract econometric model. A probability measure P_{zu} on a measurable space $Z \times U$ characterizes a population. We know that P_{zu} is an element of some space Π_{zu} of probability measures on $Z \times U$. A sample of N independent realizations of a random variable (z, u) distributed P_{zu} is drawn. We observe the realizations of z but not of u.

A parameter b in a specified parameter space B solves an equation

$$f(z, u, b) = 0 \qquad (2.30)$$

Here $f(*, *, *)$ is a given function mapping $Z \times U \times B$ into some vector space. Equation (2.30) should be interpreted as saying that almost every realization (ζ, η) of (z, u) satisfies the equation $f(\zeta, \eta, b) = 0$.

Knowledge of the function $f(*, *, *)$, the probability space Π_{zu}, and the parameter space B ostensibly derives from the findings of past theoretical and empirical research. Lack of knowledge of the values of P_{zu} and b reflects the failure of past research to yield conclusive evidence on aspects of the relationship between z and u. The estimation problem is to combine the sample data on z with the knowledge that $P_{zu} \in \Pi_{zu}$, $b \in B$, and $f(z, u, b) = 0$ so as to estimate b.

To apply the analogy principle, we need to translate the estimation problem into a form that relates b to P, the probability measure of the observable z. We show below that this is accomplished easily if $f(*, *, *)$ is separable in the unobserved variables. Models in which $f(*, *, *)$ does not enjoy such separability will be examined in Chapter 6.

2.5.2 Models separable in the unobserved variables

Let (2.30) have the form

$$u_0(z, b) - u = 0 \qquad (2.31)$$

where $u_0(*, *)$ is a given function mapping $Z \times B$ into U. Then

$$(z, u) = [z, u_0(z, b)] \tag{2.32}$$

That is, (z, u) is a function of the observable z and of the parameter b. Hence P_{zu} is determined by P and b.

Let us make the dependence of P_{zu} on (P, b) explicit. For Q in $\Pi \cup \Phi$, let $z(Q)$ denote a random variable distributed Q. For c in B, let $\psi(Q, c)$ denote the probability measure of $[z(Q), u_0\{z(Q), c\}]$. Then (2.32) implies that

$$P_{zu} = \psi(P, b) \tag{2.33}$$

By (2.33), knowing that P_{zu} is an element of Π_{zu} is the same as knowing that b satisfies the condition

$$\psi(P, b) \in \Pi_{zu} \tag{2.34}$$

This condition avoids reference to unobserved random variables. Thus, we have translated the original estimation problem into one relating b to P. The parameter space remains B. The space Π consists of all measures Q on Z such that $\psi(Q, c) \in \Pi_{zu}$ for some c in B. The translated problem is to combine the sample data on z with the knowledge that $b \in B$, $P \in \Pi$, and $\psi(P, b) \in \Pi_{zu}$ so as to estimate b.

We may now apply the analogy principle. When P_N is in Π, the analog estimate for b is

$$B_N \equiv [c \in B : \psi(P_N, c) \in \Pi_{zu}] \tag{2.35}$$

When P_N is not in Π, the analogy principle suggests selection of an estimate that makes the measure $\psi(P_N, *)$ as close as possible to Π_{zu}, in some sense.

To do this, choose a function $r(*, \Pi_{zu})$ that maps the space of probability measures on $Z \times U$ into $[0, \infty)$ and satisfies $r(\psi) = 0 \Leftrightarrow \psi \in \Pi_{zu}$. Thus, $r(*, \Pi_{zu})$ distinguishes probability measures that are in Π_{zu} from ones that are not. Then condition (2.34) is equivalent to saying that b solves the equation

$$r[\psi(P, b), \Pi_{zu}] = 0 \tag{2.36}$$

The analogy principle applied to (2.36) yields the 'closest empirical distribution' estimate

$$B_{Nr} \equiv \underset{c \in B}{\operatorname{argmin}}\, r[\psi(P_N, c), \Pi_{zu}] \tag{2.37}$$

studied in Manski (1983). In words, (2.37) selects an estimate that brings the empirical measure of $[z(P_N), u_0\{z(P_N), *\}]$ as close as possible to Π_{zu}. This estimate reduces to (2.35) when P_N is in Π. Otherwise, it depends on the chosen $r(*, \Pi_{zu})$; hence we write B_{Nr}.

2.5.3 Instrumental variables

Closest empirical distribution estimation is a recent abstraction of the method of instrumental variables, the earliest contribution of econometrics to analog estimation theory.

Wright (1928) and Reiersol (1941, 1945) independently considered the class of models in which (2.30) has the linear form

$$y(z) - x(z)'b - u = 0 \qquad (2.38)$$

Here $y(*)$ maps Z into R^1, $x(*)$ maps Z into R^K, and u is in R^1. The parameter space is R^K. The unobserved random variable u is known to be orthogonal to each of the components of a given random variable $v(z)$, where $v(*)$ maps Z into R^K. Thus, P_{zu} is known to satisfy the equation

$$\int v(z)u \, dP_{zu} = 0 \qquad (2.39)$$

Wright (1928) and Reiersol (1941) examined the problem of estimating b in the context of specific applications. A general treatment was given in Reiersol (1945). Reiersol termed $v(z)$ a set of 'instrumental variables'. He apparently thought of $v(z)$ as an instrument or tool used to learn b.

To translate this problem into a form that relates b to P, use (2.32), (2.33), and (2.38) to rewrite (2.39) as

$$\int v(z)u \, dP_{zu} = \int v(z)u \, d\psi(P, b) = \int v(z)[y(z) - x(z)'b] \, dP = 0$$

$$(2.40)$$

In his 1945 paper, Reiersol proposed analog estimation. Application of the analogy principle to (2.40) yields the instrumental variables estimate

$$B_N \equiv \left[c \in B: \int v(z)[y(z) - x(z)'c] \, dP_N = 0 \right] \qquad (2.41)$$

Since it was first proposed, the method of instrumental variables has been extended in some obvious and important respects. The modern literature does not require that $f(*, *, *)$ be linear, only that it be separable in u as in (2.31). The instrumental variable vector $v(z)$ need not be of the same length as the parameter vector b. And the available information need not be that $v(z)$ is orthogonal to u; it suffices that $v(z)$ be orthogonal to a given function of u. See Chapter 6 for details and examples.

CHAPTER 3

Regressions

The estimation of regressions is a central theme of econometrics. Let $y(*)$ and $x(*)$ be functions mapping the sample space Z into spaces Y and X respectively. In common usage, the regression of y on x refers to the expected value of $y(z)$ conditional on the realization of $x(z)$, considered as a function on X. More generally, a regression of z on x is some property of the probability measure of z conditional on the realization of $x(z)$, again considered as a function on X. This chapter applies the analogy principle to the estimation of regressions.

3.1 The estimation problem

Recall the abstract estimation problem posed at the beginning of Chapter 1. The population probability measure P is an element of a space Π of measures on Z. We observe N independent realizations of a random variable z distributed P. A parameter b in a parameter space B solves an equation $T(P, b) = 0$. The problem is to estimate b.

Within this framework, regression problems have the following structure. B is a space of functions mapping X into some space Θ. That is, for each c in B and ξ in X, $c(\xi)$ is a point in Θ. And $T(P, b) = 0$ is a collection of equations

$$S[P|\xi, b(\xi)] = 0, \qquad \xi \in X \tag{3.1}$$

Here $P|\xi$ is the probability measure P conditioned on the event $[x = \xi]$. $S(*, *)$ is a given function mapping the space $[Q|\xi, \xi \in X, Q \in \Pi] \times \Theta$ into some vector space.

3.1.1 Identification

One would like to say that the regression function $b(*)$ is identified if (3.1) has a unique zero on B. This statement is unexceptional if X is discrete with P_x, the probability measure of the random variable x, giving positive probability to every point in X. But it is problematic if, as is usual in applications, X contains subsets having probability zero under P_x. Knowledge of P does not then imply a unique collection of conditional measures $[P|\xi, \xi \in X]$.

To see this, let X_0 be a measurable subset of X with $P_x(X_0) = 0$. Let $[p_\xi, \xi \in X]$ be any collection of probability measures on Z such that $p_\xi = P|\xi$ for ξ in $X - X_0$ and $p_\xi \neq P|\xi$ for ξ in X_0. Then for every measurable set A in Z,

$$P(A) = \int_X P(A|\xi) dP_x = \int_{X - X_0} P(A|\xi) dP_x$$

$$= \int_{X - X_0} p_\xi(A) dP_x = \int_X p_\xi(A) dP_x \qquad (3.2)$$

Hence, knowledge of P does not distinguish $[P|\xi, \xi \in X]$ from $[p_\xi, \xi \in X]$.

Indeterminacy of conditional measures implies indeterminacy of regression functions. Again let X_0 be a subset of X with $P_x(X_0) = 0$. Let $c(*)$ by any element of B such that $c(\xi) = b(\xi)$ for ξ in $X - X_0$ and $c(\xi) \neq b(\xi)$ for ξ in X_0. Let $[p_\xi, \xi \in X]$ be a collection of probability measures on Z such that $p_\xi = P|\xi$ for ξ in $X - X_0$ and p_ξ solves $S[p_\xi, c(\xi)] = 0$ for ξ in X_0. Then $c(*)$ solves

$$S[p_\xi, c(\xi)] = 0, \qquad \xi \in X \qquad (3.3)$$

We cannot distinguish $[P|\xi, \xi \in X]$ from $[p_\xi, \xi \in X]$; hence we cannot distinguish $b(*)$ from $c(*)$. To summarize, $b(*)$ is not identified relative to any $c(*)$ satisfying the condition $P_x[c(\xi) \neq b(\xi)] = 0$.

The literature copes in two ways with the inherent indeterminacy of a regression function whose domain contains sets of probability zero. Often, the specification of the estimation problem excludes functions whose values differ from $b(*)$ only on sets of P_x-probability zero. Then $b(*)$ may be identified in the usual manner.

An example is the linear regression model. Let X be K-dimensional real space, let Θ be the real line, and let B be the space of linear functions on X. So $b(\xi) = \xi'\beta$ for some β in R^K and all ξ in X. Any distinct function $c(*)$ in B has the form $c(\xi) = \xi'\gamma$ for some $\gamma \neq \beta$. In this setting, $b(*)$ is identified if for every $\gamma \neq \beta$, $P_x(\xi'\gamma \neq \xi'\beta) > 0$. Thus, $b(*)$ is identified if and only if no proper subspace of X contains all the mass of P_x.

Sometimes, the specification does not exclude functions which differ from $b(*)$ only on sets of P_x-probability zero. Then it is the practice to accept a weaker definition of identification than the one we have used so far. In particular, $b(*)$ is sometimes said to be identified if, for all $c(*)$ in B,

$$[S\{P|\xi, c(\xi)\} = 0, \text{ a.e. } P_x] \Rightarrow [c(\xi) = b(\xi), \text{a.e. } P_x] \qquad (3.4)$$

An example is the Stone (1977) treatment of nonparametric regression.

3.1.2 Hyperparameters

The largest possible parameter space for a given regression problem is the space of all functions mapping X into Θ. In practice, the parameter space is usually restricted in some manner. The most familiar case is that in which B is known to be indexed by a finite-dimensional real hyperparameter.

Let Γ be a subset of R^K, let $f(*, *)$ be a given function mapping $X \times \Gamma$ into Θ, and let the parameter space have the form

$$B \equiv [f(*, \gamma), \gamma \in \Gamma] \qquad (3.5)$$

Then there exists some β in Γ such that

$$b(*) = f(*, \beta) \qquad (3.6)$$

We say that Γ indexes B and that β is a hyperparameter determining $b(*)$.

In applied regression analysis, it is common to focus attention on estimation of β rather than on estimation of $b(*)$ *per se*. This practice is easily justified if one is interested in pointwise estimation of $b(*)$ and if the functions $f(\xi, *)$, $\xi \in X$ are appropriately smooth on B. In particular, consistent estimation of β implies consistent estimation of $b(\xi)$, provided that $f(\xi, *)$ is continuous. Asymptotic normal estimation of β implies asymptotic normal estimation of $b(\xi)$, provided that $f(\xi, *)$ is continuously differentiable.

The relationship between estimation of β and uniform estimation of $b(*)$ is more subtle. Rust (1986) provides an analysis.

3.2 'Naive' analog estimation

So-called 'naive' analog estimation attempts to apply the analogy principle to the collection of equations $S[P|\xi, b(\xi)] = 0, \xi \in X$. Extend the domain of $S(*, *)$ to $\Phi \times \Theta$ and let $P_N|\xi$ denote the empirical measure P_N conditioned on the event $[x = \xi]$. The naive estimate of $b(*)$ is

$$B_N \equiv [c \in B : S\{P_N|\xi, c(\xi)\} = 0, \xi \in X] \qquad (3.7)$$

provided that B_N is non-empty. Otherwise, one selects an estimate that makes $[S\{P_N|\xi, *(\xi)\}, \xi \in X]$ as close as possible to zero, in some sense.

Naive analog estimation works well if X is finite and $P_x(\xi) > 0$ for all $\xi \in X$. As N increases, $[P_N|\xi, \xi \in X]$ converges to $[P|\xi, \xi \in X]$ in various senses. So $[S\{P_N|\xi, *(\xi)\}, \xi \in X]$ behaves well as an approximation to $[S\{P|\xi, *(\xi)\}, \xi \in X]$, provided only that $S(*, *)$ is smooth.

Naive estimation does not generally work when X contains subsets having probability zero under P_x. The empirical measure of x puts all its mass on the finite set of observed values $X_N \equiv (x_i, i = 1, \ldots, N)$. For ξ not in $X_N, P_N|\xi$ is arbitrary. For ξ in $X_N, P_N|\xi$ is determinate but does not converge to $P|\xi$ unless $P_x(\xi) > 0$. Hence, wherever $P_x(\xi) = 0$, $S[P_N|\xi, *(\xi)]$ behaves poorly as an approximation to $S[P|\xi, *(\xi)]$.

The generic failure of naive analog estimation makes it desirable to find alternative approaches. A universally useful analog estimator does not seem to exist. On the other hand, successful methods are available for important classes of regression problems. The sections that follow examine three such problems.

3.3 Method of moments estimation of moment regressions

With few exceptions, the regression problems studied in econometrics have been ones in which the regression function solves a collection of moment extremum problems or moment equations. In the former case,

$$b(\xi) - \underset{\theta \in \Theta}{\text{argmin}} \int h(z, \theta) \, dP|\xi = 0, \qquad \text{a.e. } P_x \qquad (3.8)$$

where $h(*, *)$ is a given function mapping $Z \times \Theta$ into the real line. In the latter,

$$\int g[z, b(\xi)] \, dP|\xi = 0, \qquad \text{a.e. } P_x \qquad (3.9)$$

where $g(*, *)$ is a given function mapping $Z \times \Theta$ into a real vector space.

Three classes of moment regressions will be examined in Part II. Here we stay abstract and describe the prevailing method of moments approach to estimation.

3.3.1 Moment extremum regressions

Regression problems of the moment extremum type have convenient representations which avoid reference to the collection of conditional measures $[P|\xi, \xi \in X]$.

The law of iterated expectations implies that for any function $c(*)$ mapping X into Θ,

$$\int \left[\int h\{z, c(x)\} \, dP|x \right] dP_x = \int h[z, c\{x(z)\}] \, dP \qquad (3.10)$$

It follows from (3.10) that $b(*)$ solves (3.8) on B if and only if it solves the moment extremum problem

$$b(*) - \operatorname*{argmin}_{c \in B} \int h[z, c\{x(z)\}] \, dP = 0 \qquad (3.11)$$

Application of the analogy principle to (3.11) yields a method of moments estimate for $b(*)$, namely

$$B_N = \operatorname*{argmin}_{c \in B} \int h[z, c\{x(z)\}] \, dP_N \qquad (3.12)$$

Variations on this estimate may be obtained by substituting for (3.8) an equivalent collection of problems

$$b(\xi) - \operatorname*{argmin}_{\theta \in \Theta} w(\xi) \int h(z, \theta) \, dP|\xi = 0, \qquad \text{a.e. } P_x \qquad (3.13)$$

Here $w(*)$ is a 'weighting' function mapping X into the real line with $w(\xi) > 0$, a.e. P_x. Each choice of $w(*)$ leads to a distinct estimate

$$B_{Nw} = \operatorname*{argmin}_{c \in B} \int w\{x(z)\} h[z, c\{x(z)\}] \, dP_N \qquad (3.14)$$

3.3.2 Moment equation regressions

We can similarly transform the collection of moment equations (3.9) into a single moment equation relating b to P. Here, however, we must be careful. The derived moment equation may not preserve the information available in the original regression problem.

By the law of iterated expectations,

$$\int \left[\int g\{z, c(x)\} \, dP|x \right] dP_x = \int g[z, c\{x(z)\}] \, dP \qquad (3.15)$$

It follows that any solution to (3.9) solves the moment equation

$$\int g[z, b\{x(z)\}] \, dP = 0 \qquad (3.16)$$

The converse may or may not hold. Solution of (3.16) does not always imply solution of the collection of problems

$$\int g[z, b(\xi)] \, dP|\xi = 0, \qquad \text{a.e. } P_x \qquad (3.17)$$

It may rather be that averaged with respect to P_x, positive and negative values of the expression $\int g[z, b(\xi)] \, dP|\xi$ balance. If so, the derived moment equation (3.16) fails to identify the regression function.

Suppose that, in the problem of interest, (3.16) does identify the regression function. Then one may contemplate application of the analogy principle to (3.16). Selecting an origin-preserving transformation $r(*)$ and minimizing the sample analog of $r[\int g\{z, *(x(z))\} \, dP]$ on B yields a method of moments estimate

$$B_{Nr} = \operatorname*{argmin}_{c \in B} r\left[\int g\{z, c(x(z))\} \, dP_N \right] \qquad (3.18)$$

Again, variations may be obtained by introducing a weighting function.

3.3.3 *The parameter space*

The estimates (3.12) and (3.18) are well defined whatever the specification of the parameter space. Statistical properties, however, vary with the parameter space. Method of moments estimation of regression functions works well when B is a sufficiently small space of functions but breaks down when B is too large. To see this, let us consider the estimate (3.12) under two polar specifications.

First, let B be a space of functions indexed by a K-dimensional real hyperparameter. Thus, let Γ be a subset of R^K, let $f(*, *)$ be a given function mapping $X \times \Gamma$ into Θ, and let the parameter space be

$$B \equiv [f(*, \gamma), \gamma \in \Gamma] \tag{3.19}$$

Then the method of moments estimate of $b(*)$ is

$$B_N = [f(*, \gamma), \gamma \in \Gamma_N] \tag{3.20}$$

where

$$\Gamma_N \equiv \underset{\gamma \in \Gamma}{\text{argmin}} \int h[z, f\{x(z), \gamma\}] \, dP_N \tag{3.21}$$

Given modest regularity conditions, Γ_N and B_N are well-behaved estimates of the hyperparameter and of $b(*)$ respectively.

Second, let B the space of all functions mapping X into Θ. That is, let the parameter space be the Cartesian product

$$B \equiv (\times \Theta, \xi \in X) \tag{3.22}$$

Let P_{Nx} denote the empirical measure of x and let X_N denote its support. The method of moments estimate of $b(*)$ is the Cartesian product set

$$B_N = (\times B_N(\xi), \xi \in X) \tag{3.23}$$

where

$$B_N(\xi) = \underset{\theta \in \Theta}{\text{argmin}} \int h(z, \theta) \, dP_N | \xi \qquad \text{for } \xi \text{ in } X_N \tag{3.24a}$$

and

$$B_N(\xi) = \Theta \qquad \text{for } \xi \text{ in } X - X_N \tag{3.24b}$$

That is, B_N is the set of all functions solving (3.24a) at each ξ in the support and taking arbitrary values elsewhere. Except in the special case where $P_x(\xi) > 0$, $B_N(\xi)$ does not generally converge to $b(\xi)$. Hence, B_N does not generally converge to b.

Does the method of moments work when the parameter space restricts $b(*)$ but cannot be indexed by a finite-dimensional hyperparameter? Our negative finding for $B = (\times \Theta, \xi \in X)$ remains in force whenever the available information restricts the behavior of $b(*)$ only locally.

We say that B restricts $b(*)$ only locally if, given any finite set A in X and any set $(\theta_\xi, \xi \in A)$ in Θ, there is some function $c(*)$ in B such that $c(\xi) = \theta_\xi$ for ξ in A. An important class of specifications that restrict $b(*)$ only locally are those in which $b(*)$ is known to be a smooth function, say a k-times differentiable function. Given any finite A and $(\theta_\xi, \xi \in A)$, there always exists a k-times differentiable function that passes through the points (ξ, θ_ξ), $\xi \in A$.

To see that the method of moments breaks down when B restricts $b(*)$ only locally, let X_N be the finite set A. For ξ in X_N, let θ_ξ be any element of $B_N(\xi)$, where $B_N(\xi)$ was defined in (3.24a). Then B contains some function that passes through the points (ξ, θ_ξ), $\xi \in X_N$. Any such function minimizes $\int h[z, *\{x(z)\}] dP_N$ on $(\times \Theta, \xi \in X)$, hence on B.

We may conclude that if method of moments estimation of regressions is to succeed, the parameter space must, in general, restrict $b(*)$ more than locally. Finite-dimensional parameter spaces certainly do this. The literature on 'isotonic regression' gives an example of a non-finite dimensional restriction that suffices. Here, X is the real line and B is the space of monotone functions on X. See Barlow *et al.* (1972) and Robertson and Wright (1975).

It is important to understand that the failure of the method of moments to be consistent when B is too large a space of functions does not indicate that $b(*)$ is unidentified. We have noted earlier that the moment problem (3.11) inherits the identification properties of the original regression problem (3.8). The difficulty with the method of moments is rather that on a large domain, the function $\int h[z, *\{x(z)\}] dP_N$ does not behave like $\int h[z, *\{x(z)\}] dP$, even as $N \to \infty$.

3.4 Kernel estimation of conditional density functions

Section 2.2 applied the analogy principle to the problem of nonparametric density estimation. The kernel method derived there can be used to estimate conditional density functions as well.

As before, let Z be K-dimensional real space and let Π be the space of all probability measures on R^K that are absolutely continuous with respect to Lebesgue measure. Let $z = (y, x)$, where y takes values in R^I, x in R^J, and $I + J = K$. Let $P_y|\xi$ denote the probability measure of y conditional on the event $[x = \xi]$. Let $\varphi_\mu(*, P_y|\xi)$ denote the density of y conditional on this event.

The problem is to estimate the conditional densities $\varphi_\mu(*, P_y|\xi)$, a.e. P_x in the absence of restrictions. Thus, the parameter b is a function on $R^I \times R^J$ solving the collection of equations

$$b(*, \xi) - \varphi_\mu(*, P_y|\xi) = 0, \qquad \text{a.e. } P_x \qquad (3.25)$$

To estimate $b(*, *)$, we first find an alternative representation of (3.25) and then apply the analogy principle.

It suffices to consider those ξ in X at which P_x has positive density. For each such ξ, the conditional density $\varphi_\mu(*, P_y | \xi)$ can be written as the ratio of the density of (y, x) evaluated at $(*, \xi)$ to the density of x evaluated at ξ. That is,

$$\varphi_\mu(*, P_y | \xi) = \frac{\varphi_\mu[(*, \xi), P]}{\varphi_\mu(\xi, P_x)} \qquad (3.26)$$

Let $\sigma(*)$ and $\sigma_x(*)$ be chosen smoothing functions defined on the spaces of probability measures on R^K and R^J. Let G and G_x be chosen absolutely continuous probability measures on R^K and R^J. Let $g(*)$ and $g_x(*)$ be the respective density functions. Then $\varphi_\mu[(*, \xi), P] = \varphi_\mu[(*, \xi), P \oplus \sigma(P)G]$ and $\varphi_\mu(\xi, P_x) = \varphi_\mu[\xi, P_x \oplus \sigma_x(P_x)G_x]$. Hence,

$$b(*, \xi) - \frac{\varphi_\mu[(*, \xi), P \oplus \sigma(P)G]}{\varphi_\mu[\xi, P_x \oplus \sigma_x(P_x)G_x]} = 0 \qquad (3.27)$$

Application of the analogy principle to (3.27) yields the kernel conditional density estimate

$$b_N(*, \xi) \equiv \frac{1/\sigma(P_N)^K \dfrac{1}{N} \sum_{i=1}^N g[\{(*, \xi) - (y_i, x_i)\}/\sigma(P_N)]}{1/\sigma_x(P_{Nx})^J \dfrac{1}{N} \sum_{i=1}^N g_x[(\xi - x_i)/\sigma_x(P_{Nx})]} \qquad (3.28)$$

Having an estimate of the conditional density $\varphi_\mu(*, P_y | \xi)$, one may derive an estimate of functions of this density. For example, the kernel conditional density estimate may be used to estimate the mean regression of y on x. By definition,

$$E(y | \xi) \equiv \int y \varphi_\mu(y, P_y | \xi) \, d\mu \qquad (3.29)$$

The kernel estimate is

$$E_N(y | \xi) \equiv \int y b_N(y, \xi) \, d\mu \qquad (3.30)$$

Prakasa Rao (1983, Section 4.2) collects findings from the literature studying the asymptotic properties of the estimate (3.30).

3.5 Smallest neighborhood estimation of conditional probability measures

Consider the problem of estimating the collection of conditional probability measures $P | \xi, \xi \in X$, in the absence of restrictions. That is, let $b(*)$ map X into the space of all probability measures on Z and solve the collection of equations

$$b(\xi) - P|\xi = 0, \qquad \xi \in X \tag{3.31}$$

The naive estimate $P_N|\xi$, $\xi \in X$ can work only if X is discrete. The kernel method may be applied if P is absolutely continuous but not otherwise. Here we seek an estimator that works whether or not X is discrete and whether or not P is absolutely continuous.

To obtain such a method, we introduce an alternative representation of (3.31). In short, we replace probability measures conditioning on events of probability zero by ones that condition on neighborhoods having vanishingly small positive probability. This done, application of the analogy principle works. We term the resulting analog method 'smallest neighborhood' estimation.

3.5.1 *Representation of the problem*

Select a metric ρ on the space X. Select a continuous, strictly increasing function $m(*)$ mapping $[0, \infty)$ into $[0, \infty)$ with $m(0) = 0$ and $m(d) > d$ for $d > 0$. For ξ in X and $d \geqslant 0$, define

$$X(\xi, d) \equiv [\xi' \in X : \rho(\xi, \xi') \leqslant d] \tag{3.32}$$

$$d(\xi, P_x) \equiv \inf d : P_x[X(\xi, d)] > 0 \tag{3.33}$$

and

$$A(\xi, P_x) \equiv X[\xi, m\{d(\xi, P_x)\}] \tag{3.34}$$

That is, $X(\xi, d)$ is the closed ball of radius d centered at ξ and $d(\xi, P_x)$ is the infimum of d such that $X(\xi, d)$ has positive probability under P_x. The set $A(\xi, P_x)$ is the closed ball of radius $m\{d(\xi, P_x)\}$ centered at ξ.

Now replace the regression problem (3.31) with

$$b(\xi) - P|A(\xi, P_x) = 0, \qquad \xi \in X \tag{3.35}$$

Here, $P|A(\xi, P_x)$ is the probability measure P conditioned on the event that x is within distance $m\{d(\xi, P_x)\}$ of ξ. Substitution of (3.35) for (3.31) leaves the estimation problem unchanged.

To see this, let X_s be the support of P_x. That is,

$$X_s \equiv [\xi \in X : P_x[X(\xi, d)] > 0, \forall d > 0] \tag{3.36}$$

It follows from (3.32) through (3.34) that

$$\xi \in X_s \Rightarrow d(\xi, P_x) = 0 \Rightarrow m\{d(\xi, P_x)\} = 0$$
$$\Rightarrow A(\xi, P_x) = \{\xi\} \Rightarrow P|A(\xi, P_x) = P|\xi \tag{3.37}$$

It remains to consider ξ not in X_s. In general, $P|A(\xi, P_x)$ need not equal $P|\xi$ for such ξ. But the set of non-support points necessarily has probability zero. See Chung (1974, p. 31). Therefore,

$$P|A(\xi, P_x) = P|\xi, \qquad \text{a.e. } P_x \qquad (3.38)$$

In light of our discussion of identification, this means that (3.31) and (3.35) are equivalent.

3.5.2 Smallest neighborhood estimates

A smallest neighborhood estimate is obtained by applying the analogy principle to (3.35). Thus,

$$b_N(\xi) \equiv P_N|A(\xi, P_{Nx}), \qquad \xi \in X \qquad (3.39)$$

The expression $P_N|A(\xi, P_{Nx})$ has a simple interpretation. $d(\xi, P_{Nx})$ is the distance from ξ to its nearest neighbor among the N observations of x. So $X[\xi, d(\xi, P_{Nx})]$ is the smallest closed neighborhood of ξ having positive empirical probability. And $A(\xi, P_{Nx})$ is this neighborhood 'blown up' to radius $m\{d(\xi, P_{Nx})\}$.

When ξ is among the sample realizations of $x(z)$, the distance from ξ to its nearest sample neighbor is zero. Hence $P_N|A(\xi, P_{Nx}) = P_N|\xi$, as in naive estimation. When ξ is not among the sample realizations, this distance is positive. Then $P_N|A(\xi, P_{Nx})$ is the empirical measure P_N conditioned on the event that x is within distance $m\{d(\xi, P_{Nx})\}$ of ξ.

3.5.3 Smallest neighborhood estimation of mean regressions

Given an estimate of $P|\xi$, $\xi \in X$, one may derive an estimate of any regression function. For example, the smallest neighborhood method may be used to estimate the mean regression of y on x. Let $b(*)$ solve the collection of equations

$$b(\xi) - \int y(z)\, dP|\xi = 0, \qquad \xi \in X \qquad (3.40)$$

Substitute for (3.40) the equivalent collection of equations

$$b(\xi) - \int y(z)\, dP|A(\xi, P_x) = 0, \qquad \xi \in X \qquad (3.41)$$

The smallest neighborhood estimate of the mean regression function is

$$b_N(\xi) \equiv \int y(z) \, dP_N | A(\xi, P_{Nx}) = \frac{1}{N(\xi, P_{Nx})} \sum_{i \in I(\xi, N)} y(z_i) \qquad (3.42)$$

Here $N(\xi, P_{Nx})$ is the number of sample observations of z for which $x(z)$ is in $A(\xi, P_{Nx})$ and $I(\xi, N)$ indexes these observations.

An Appendix to this section proves that the estimate (3.42) is pointwise consistent, provided that the function $m(*)$ is chosen appropriately and that P is minimally regular. Some $m(*)$ that work are the power functions

$$m(d) = d + \alpha_1 d^{\alpha_2} \qquad (3.43)$$

for $0 < \alpha_1 < \infty$ and $0 < \alpha_2 < 1$.

3.5.4 *The nearest neighbor and histogram methods*

Smallest neighborhood estimation is reminiscent of, but distinct from, the nearest neighbor and histogram methods for estimating conditional probability measures. All three approaches impose a metric on X and estimate $P|\xi$ by the empirical measure of z conditioned on the event that x is within some neighborhood of ξ. They differ in the way this neighborhood is determined.

In nearest neighbor estimation, a positive integer $k(N)$, dependent on the sample size N, is chosen by the researcher. Then $P|\xi$ is estimated by P_N conditioned on the event that x is among the k nearest sample neighbors to ξ. So the number of observations used to estimate $P|\xi$ is predetermined and the neighborhood of ξ that contains these observations is random.

In histogram estimation, a neighborhood radius $\delta(N)$, dependent on N, is chosen. Then $P|\xi$ is estimated by $P_N | X[\xi, \delta(N)]$. Here, the number of observations used to estimate $P|\xi$ is random and the neighborhood that contains these observations is predetermined.

In smallest neighborhood estimation, a function $m(*)$ is chosen. When $m(*)$ is evaluated at the random distance $d(\xi, P_{Nx})$ from ξ to its nearest sample neighbor, a random neighborhood $A(\xi, P_{Nx})$ results. The number of observations within $A(\xi, P_{Nx})$ is random but always positive.

It would be of interest to know whether the nearest neighbor and histogram methods can be derived as analog estimates. I am not aware of representations of conditional probability measures that yield these methods. See Prakasa Rao (1983) for further details on nearest neighbor and histogram estimation.

3.5.5 kth-smallest neighborhood estimation

Smallest neighborhood estimation has one mildly irritating feature not shared by the nearest neighbor and histogram methods. Fix ξ in X. We pointed out earlier that if ξ is among the sample realizations of x, the smallest neighborhood estimate of $P|\xi$ is $P_N|\xi$. This is desirable if $P_x(\xi) > 0$ but not otherwise.

The equivalence of the smallest neighborhood and naive estimates on the sample realizations of x is innocuous for the pointwise consistency of smallest neighborhood estimates. Given any ξ with $P_x(\xi) = 0$, there is probability zero that ξ ever appears among the observations of x. The irritant is, rather, that smallest neighborhood estimates are not uniformly consistent on X.

A simple remedy is 'kth-smallest neighborhood estimation'. Select a positive integer k. Let $d_{Nk}(\xi)$ be the distance from ξ to its kth-nearest neighbor among the N observations of x. Let $A_{Nk}(\xi) \equiv X[\xi, m\{d_{Nk}(\xi)\}]$. Now let $P_N|A_{Nk}(\xi)$ define the kth-smallest neighborhood estimate of $P|\xi$.

A kth-smallest neighborhood estimate of $P|\xi$ reduces to the naive estimate only if k or more sample realizations of x have the value ξ. With probability one, there exists no ξ with $P_x(\xi) = 0$ such that more than one observation of x has the value ξ. Hence, with probability one, kth-smallest neighborhood estimation does not misbehave anywhere, provided that k is chosen to be larger than one.

I am not aware of a representation of $P|\xi$ for which $P|A_{Nk}(\xi), k > 1$ is the sample analog. The integer k refers to a number of sample realizations of x. For $k > 1$, the distance to the kth-nearest neighbor of ξ is not determined by the empirical measure P_{Nx} alone. The case $k = 1$ is special. The distance to the nearest neighbor is the same as the radius of the smallest neighborhood having positive empirical probability.

Appendix to 3.5:   Consistency of smallest neighborhood estimates of mean regressions

The smallest neighborhood estimate of a mean regression function

$b(*)$, given in (3.42), is restated below:

$$b_N(\xi) \equiv \int y(z)\, dP_N | A(\xi, P_{Nx}) = \frac{1}{N(\xi, P_{Nx})} \sum_{i \in I(\xi, N)} y(z_i) \quad (3.44)$$

The theorem that follows gives conditions that are sufficient for pointwise weak consistency of this estimate. Three lemmas then show that these conditions are satisfied if $m(*)$ is selected appropriately, provided only that P be minimally regular.

Consistency Theorem
Let $y(*)$ map Z into the real line. Fix $\xi \in X$. Assume that the following conditions hold:

[1a] $\xi' \to \xi \Rightarrow E(y|\xi') \to E(y|\xi)$.
[1b] $\exists d_0 > 0$ and $\lambda > 0$ s.t. Var $(y|x = \xi') \leqslant \lambda$ for $\xi' \in X(\xi, d_0)$.
[1c] As $N \to \infty$, $d(\xi, P_{Nx}) \to 0$ in probability.
[1d] As $N \to \infty$, $N(\xi, P_{Nx}) \to \infty$ in probability.

Then as $N \to \infty$, $\int y(z)\, dP_N | A(\xi, P_{Nx}) \to E(y|\xi)$ in probability.   ∎

PROOF Conditional on the empirical measure of x, the mean and variance of $b_N(\xi)$ are, provided that the relevant terms exist,

$$E[b_N(\xi)|P_{Nx}] = \frac{1}{N(\xi, P_{Nx})} \sum_{i \in I(\xi, N)} b(x_i) \quad (3.45)$$

and

$$\text{Var}\,[b_N(\xi)|P_{Nx}] = \frac{1}{N(\xi, P_{Nx})^2} \sum_{i \in I(\xi, N)} \text{Var}(y|x = x_i) \quad (3.46)$$

where $x_i = x(z_i)$.
   Condition [1a] implies that given any $\eta > 0$, there exists $d_\eta > 0$ such that

$$x_i \in X(\xi, d_\eta) \Rightarrow |b(x_i) - b(\xi)| < \eta \quad (3.47)$$

Recall that $A(\xi, P_{Nx}) \equiv X[\xi, m\{d(\xi, P_{Nx})\}]$. Hence,

$$E[b_N(\xi)|P_{Nx}, d(\xi, P_{Nx}) < m^{-1}(d_\eta)] \in [b(\xi) - \eta, b(\xi) + \eta] \quad (3.48)$$

Condition [1b] implies that the variances Var$(y|x = x_i)$, $i \in I(\xi, N)$ are bounded by λ, provided that $A(\xi, P_{Nx}) \subset X(\xi, d_0)$. Hence,

$$\text{Var}\,[b_N(\xi)|P_{Nx}, d(\xi, P_{Nx}) < m^{-1}(d_0)] \leqslant \frac{\lambda}{N(\xi, P_{Nx})} \quad (3.49)$$

Now let $0 < \delta < \min[m^{-1}(d_\eta), m^{-1}(d_0)]$ and let $0 < J < \infty$. Consider the mean and variance of $b_N(\xi)$ conditional on the sample size and on the event that the empirical measure of x is a member of the set of measures

$$C(\delta, J) \equiv [Q_x : d(\xi, Q_x) < \delta \cap N(\xi, Q_x) > J] \tag{3.50}$$

It follows from (3.48) that for all feasible δ and J,

$$E_{N\delta J} \equiv E[b_N(\xi) | P_{Nx} \in C(\delta, J)] \in [b(\xi) - \eta, b(\xi) + \eta] \tag{3.51}$$

It follows from (3.48) and (3.49) that

$$\begin{aligned}
V_{N\delta J} &\equiv \text{Var}\,[b_N(\xi) | P_{Nx} \in C(\delta, J)] \\
&= \text{Var}\,[E[b_N(\xi) | P_{Nx}, d(\xi, P_{Nx}) < m^{-1}(\delta)] | P_{Nx} \in C(\delta, J)] \\
&\quad + E[\text{Var}\,[b_N(\xi) | P_{Nx}, d(\xi, P_{Nx}) < m^{-1}(\delta)] | P_{Nx} \in C(\delta, J)] \\
&\leqslant 4\eta^2 + \lambda/J \tag{3.52}
\end{aligned}$$

Chebychev's inequality and (3.52) imply that for any $v > 0$,

$$\begin{aligned}
\text{Prob}\,[|b_N(\xi) - E_{N\delta J}| < v | P_{Nx} \in C(\delta, J)] &> 1 - V_{N\delta J}/v^2 \\
&\geqslant 1 - (4\eta^2 + \lambda/J)/v^2
\end{aligned} \tag{3.53}$$

Hence, by (3.51)

$$\text{Prob}\,[|b_N(\xi) - b(\xi)| < \eta + v | P_{Nx} \in C(\delta, J)] > 1 - (4\eta^2 + \lambda/J)/v^2 \tag{3.54}$$

Finally, remove the conditioning on $C(\delta, J)$. In general,

$$\begin{aligned}
&\text{Prob}\,[|b_N(\xi) - b(\xi)| < \eta + v] \\
&= \text{Prob}\,[|b_N(\xi) - b(\xi)| < \eta + v | P_{Nx} \in C(\delta, J)] \\
&\quad \times \text{Prob}\,[P_{Nx} \in C(\delta, J)] \\
&\quad + \text{Prob}\,[|b_N(\xi) - b(\xi)| < \eta + v | P_{Nx} \notin C(\delta, J)] \times \text{Prob}\,[P_{Nx} \notin C(\delta, J)]
\end{aligned} \tag{3.55}$$

Conditions [1c] and [1d] imply that as $N \to \infty$,

$$\text{Prob}[P_{Nx} \in C(\delta, J)] \to 1 \tag{3.56}$$

This and (3.55) imply that

$$\liminf_{N \to \infty} \text{Prob}\,[|b_N(\xi) - b(\xi)| < \eta + v] \geqslant 1 - (4\eta^2 + \lambda/J)/v^2 \tag{3.57}$$

Now let $\eta \to 0$ and $J \to \infty$. By (3.57), $\text{Prob}\,[|b_N(\xi) - b(\xi)| < v] \to 1$ for every $v > 0$.   Q.E.D.

The four conditions of this theorem are unsurprising. Smallest neighborhood estimates, like histogram and nearest neighbor estimates, approximate the conditional mean by a local average. For a local average to be consistent, the population must be sufficiently regular. Conditions [1a] and [1b] suffice. That is, it is enough that $E(y|*)$ be continuous at ξ and that, for ξ' near ξ, the variances of the measures $P|\xi'$ be bounded.

Given these regularity conditions on P, the local average converges if conditions [1c] and [1d] hold. That is, as $N \to \infty$, the neighborhood of ξ on which the average is taken should shrink toward ξ and, at the same time, the average should be computed on increasingly many observations.

Selection of $m(*)$

There is a tension between conditions [1c] and [1d]. To make the consistency theorem operational, we need to show that it is possible to select $m(*)$ so that both [1c] and [1d] hold.

To do this, we work with the distribution $G_\xi(*)$ of the distance of the random variable x to the point $\xi \in X$. That is, for $d \geqslant 0$, define

$$G_\xi(d) \equiv P_x[\rho(\xi, x) \leqslant d] \equiv P_x[X(\xi, d)] \tag{3.58}$$

By the Lebesgue decomposition theorem, the probability measure on $[0, \infty)$ generated by G_ξ can be decomposed uniquely into the sum of a discrete measure, a singular continuous measure, and a measure that is absolutely continuous with respect to Lebesgue measure. See Chung (1974, p. 12). Let $g_\xi(*)$ denote the density of the absolutely continuous component.

With this as background, we have the following results.

Lemma 1

Let ξ be in the support X_s of P_x. Let $N \to \infty$. Then $d(\xi, P_{Nx}) \to 0$ in probability. ■

PROOF $d(\xi, P_{Nx})$ is the distance from ξ to its nearest neighbor among the N observations of x. By (3.58) and the assumption of random sampling,

$$\text{Prob}[d(\xi, P_{Nx}) \leqslant \delta] = 1 - [1 - G_\xi(\delta)]^N \tag{3.59}$$

for $\delta \geqslant 0$. By the definition of X_s in (3.36), $G_\xi(\delta) > 0$ for all $\delta > 0$.

Hence, for all $\delta > 0$, $\text{Prob}[d(\xi, P_{Nx}) \leqslant \delta] \to 1$ as $N \to \infty$.   Q.E.D.

Lemma 2

Assume that $P_x(\xi) > 0$. Let $N \to \infty$. Then $N(\xi, P_{Nx}) \to \infty$ almost surely. ∎

PROOF By the strong law of large numbers, $P_{Nx}(\xi) \to P_x(\xi) > 0$ almost surely. Let $0 < \eta < P_x(\xi)$. Then with probability one, there exists a finite N_0 such that $N > N_0 \Rightarrow P_{Nx}(\xi) > \eta$. But $P_{Nx}(\xi) > \eta \Rightarrow d(\xi, P_{Nx}) = 0 \Rightarrow A(\xi, P_{Nx}) = \{\xi\} \Rightarrow N(\xi, P_{Nx}) = NP_{Nx}(\xi) > N\eta$.   QE.D.

Lemma 3

Assume that for some $d_1 > 0$, $G_\xi(d_1) = \int_0^{d_1} g_\xi(\delta)\,d\delta$. Moreover, $g_1 \leqslant g_\xi(\delta) \leqslant g_2$ for $\delta \leqslant d_1$, where $0 < g_1 < g_2 < \infty$. Let $m(*)$ be differentiable with derivative $m_1(*)$ satisfying the conditions $m_1(\delta) \geqslant 1$, all δ, and $m_1(\delta) \to \infty$ as $\delta \to 0$. Then $N(\xi, P_{Nx}) \to \infty$ in probability. ∎

PROOF Let J be any positive integer. The lemma states that as $N \to \infty$, $\text{Prob}[N(\xi, P_{Nx}) < J] \to 0$. But

$$\text{Prob}[N(\xi, P_{Nx}) < J] = \sum_{j=0}^{J-1} \text{Prob}[N(\xi, P_{Nx}) = j] \qquad (3.60)$$

By construction, $N(\xi, P_{Nx}) \geqslant 1$ always. Hence, it suffices to show that as $N \to \infty$, $\text{Prob}[N(\xi, P_{Nx}) = j] \to 0$ for each positive integer j.
  For any $d > 0$,

$$\begin{aligned}
\text{Prob}[N(\xi, P_{Nx}) &= j] \\
&= \text{Prob}[N(\xi, P_{Nx}) = j \cap d(\xi, P_{Nx}) \leqslant d] \\
&\quad + \text{Prob}[N(\xi, P_{Nx}) = j \cap d(\xi, P_{Nx}) > d] \\
&\leqslant \text{Prob}[N(\xi, P_{Nx}) = j \cap d(\xi, P_{Nx}) \leqslant d] \\
&\quad + \text{Prob}[d(\xi, P_{Nx}) > d] \qquad\qquad (3.61)
\end{aligned}$$

By assumption, $g_\xi(*) > 0$ in a neighborhood of zero. So $\xi \in X_s$. Hence, by Lemma 1, $\text{Prob}[d(\xi, P_{Nx}) > d] \to 0$. Therefore, we need only to show that $\text{Prob}[N(\xi, P_{Nx}) = j \cap d(\xi, P_{Nx}) \leqslant d] \to 0$. In particular, it suffices to choose $d_2 = m^{-1}(d_1)$ and show that $\text{Prob}[N(\xi, P_{Nx}) = j \cap d(\xi, P_{Nx}) \leqslant d_2] \to 0$.
  Observe that

$$d(\xi, P_{Nx}) = \min_{i=1,\dots,N} \rho(\xi, x_i) \qquad (3.62)$$

That is, $d(\xi, P_{Nx})$ is the first order statistic in a random sample of size N from G_ξ. Also, $N(\xi, P_{Nx}) = j$ if and only if the jth order statistic is less than or equal to $m[d(\xi, P_{Nx})]$ and the $(j+1)$st is greater than $m[d(\xi, P_{Nx})]$. By assumption, the mass of G_ξ in the interval $[0, d_1]$ derives entirely from the absolutely continuous component of G_ξ. It follows that

$$\text{Prob}[N(\xi, P_{Nx}) = j \cap d(\xi, P_{Nx}) \leqslant d_2]$$

$$= \int_0^{d_2} N g_\xi(\delta) \frac{(N-1)!}{(j-1)!(N-j)!}$$
$$\times \left[G_\xi[m(\delta)] - G_\xi(\delta) \right]^{j-1} \left[1 - G_\xi[m(\delta)] \right]^{N-j} d\delta$$

$$\leqslant \int_0^{d_2} N g_\xi(\delta) \frac{(N-1)!}{(j-1)!(N-j)!} \left[G_\xi[m(\delta)] \right]^{j-1}$$
$$\times \left[1 - G_\xi[m(\delta)] \right]^{N-j} d\delta \tag{3.63}$$

Thus, it suffices to show that as $N \to \infty$,

$$\int_0^{d_2} N g_\xi(\delta) \frac{(N-1)!}{(j-1)!(N-j)!} \left[G_\xi[m(\delta)] \right]^{j-1} \left[1 - G_\xi[m(\delta)] \right]^{(N-j)} d\delta \to 0 \tag{3.64}$$

The integrand in (3.64) is closely related to the density of the jth order statistic of a random sample of N observations drawn from the distribution function $G_\xi[m(*)]$. Continuity and strict monotonicity of $m(*)$ imply that $G_\xi[m(*)]$ is a legitimate distribution function. Differentiability of $m(*)$ implies that the absolutely continuous component of $G_\xi[m(*)]$ has density $g_\xi[m(*)]m_1(*)$. Hence, the density at δ of the absolutely continuous component of the distribution of the jth order statistic from $G_\xi[m(*)]$ is (see Lehmann, 1983, p. 353).

$$\varphi_{\xi j N}(\delta) \equiv N g_\xi[m(\delta)] m_1(\delta)$$

$$\times \frac{(N-1)!}{(j-1)!(N-j)!} \left[G_\xi[m(\delta)] \right]^{j-1} \left[1 - G_\xi[m(\delta)] \right]^{(N-j)} \tag{3.65}$$

It follows that (3.64) is equivalent to the condition

$$\int_0^{d_2} \varphi_{\xi j N}(\delta) \frac{g_\xi(\delta)}{g_\xi[m(\delta)] m_1(\delta)} d\delta \to 0 \tag{3.66}$$

By assumption, $0 < g_1 \leqslant g_\xi(\delta) \leqslant g_2 < \infty$ for $\delta \leqslant d_1$. Hence, (3.66) is equivalent to

$$\int_0^{d_2} \varphi_{\xi j N}(\delta) \frac{1}{m_1(\delta)} d\delta \to 0 \qquad (3.67)$$

Also by assumption, $m_1(\delta) \to \infty$ as $\delta \to 0$. Hence, given any $\varepsilon > 0$, there exists a $\delta_\varepsilon > 0$ such that $\delta \leqslant \delta_\varepsilon \Rightarrow m_1(\delta) > \varepsilon$. Let $d_\varepsilon \equiv \min(d_2, \delta_\varepsilon)$. Then

$$\begin{aligned}
\int_0^{d_2} \varphi_{\xi j N}(\delta) \frac{1}{m_1(\delta)} d\delta &= \int_0^{d_\varepsilon} \varphi_{\xi j N}(\delta) \frac{1}{m_1(\delta)} d\delta \\
&\quad + \int_{d_\varepsilon}^{d_2} \varphi_{\xi j N}(\delta) \frac{1}{m_1(\delta)} d\delta \\
&\leqslant \frac{1}{\varepsilon} \int_0^{d_\varepsilon} \varphi_{\xi j N}(\delta) d\delta + \int_{d_\varepsilon}^{d_2} \varphi_{\xi j N}(\delta) d\delta \qquad (3.68)
\end{aligned}$$

As $N \to \infty$, the jth order statistic of a sample of size N from $G_\xi[m(*)]$ approaches zero with probability one. Hence,

$$\int_0^{d_\varepsilon} \varphi_{\xi j N}(\delta) d\delta \to 1 \qquad (3.69)$$

and

$$\int_{d_\varepsilon}^{d_2} \varphi_{\xi j N}(\delta) d\delta \to 0 \qquad (3.70)$$

It follows that the left-hand side of (3.68) is asymptotically bounded above by $1/\varepsilon$. Letting $\varepsilon \to \infty$ completes the proof. Q.E.D.

Lemma 1 states that condition [1c] holds if ξ is in the support of P_x. Lemma 2 says that condition [1d] holds if P_x places positive mass at ξ. Lemma 3 addresses a much more subtle question. Can $m(*)$ be chosen so that condition [1d] is satisfied when ξ is in the support of P_x but P_x places zero mass at ξ?

We obtain a positive answer provided only that $G_\xi(*)$ is well-behaved in a neighborhood of zero. It suffices that in a neighborhood of zero, the density $g_\xi(*)$ of the absolutely continuous component of $G_\xi(*)$ be bounded away from zero and infinity. The lemma also assumes that $G_\xi(*)$ has no singular continuous component in a neighborhood of zero but this condition is inessential.

We find that condition [1d] is satisfied if $m(*)$ is a function whose derivative $m_1(\delta) \to \infty$ as $\delta \to 0$. This property is essential. It can be shown that if $m_1(\delta)$ stays bounded as $\delta \to 0$, then $N(\xi, P_{Nx})$ stays bounded with positive probability.

One class of functions $m(*)$ that work are the power functions

$$m(d) = d + \alpha_1 d^{\alpha_2} \qquad (3.71)$$

for $0 < \alpha_1 < \infty$ and $0 < \alpha_2 < 1$. Here, $m_1(d) = 1 + \alpha_1 \alpha_2 d^{\alpha_2 - 1}$.

Given that all $m(*)$ of the form (3.71) yield consistent estimates, one would like guidance on the selection of the constants (α_1, α_2). More generally, one would like a criterion for selection of $m(*)$ from the space of all functions that satisfy the assumptions of Lemma 3. This question, which will not be pursued here, resembles questions that arise in nearest neighbor and histogram estimation. There, the analyst must decide how to increase the number of neighbors or shrink the window width as $N \to \infty$. Here, the problem of selecting a function whose argument is the sample size is replaced by one of selecting a function whose argument is the distance to the nearest neighbor.

PART II

Moment problems

The three chapters of Part II describe estimation problems prominent in econometric research. Chapter 4 presents the problem of best conditional prediction. Chapter 5 examines conditional likelihood problems. Chapter 6 studies the estimation of econometric models.

The estimation problems treated here vary in substance but share a common formal structure. Each can be represented as a moment regression. So parameters of prediction problems, likelihood problems, and econometric models are all estimable by a common analog estimator, the method of moments.

The chapters of Part II specify estimation problems and derive method of moments estimates. These chapters emphasize basic ideas and, to the extent possible, avoid burdening the discussion with technical detail. Part III will develop asymptotic theory for method of moment estimation. There, we shall have to pay closer attention to the specification of the parameter and sample spaces and to regularity conditions.

CHAPTER 4

Conditional prediction problems

A conditional prediction problem presumes that one observes a realization of a random variable x and wishes to predict the realization of some other random variable y. A best predictor of y conditional on x is a prediction that minimizes expected loss with respect to a specified loss function.

The estimation of best predictors may be the most extensively studied of all regression problems. One reason is, simply enough, that prediction problems often arise in practice. Another, quite different, reason is that best predictors are useful summary statistics characterizing the location of a random variable.

Section 4.1 describes the generic properties of conditional prediction problems. Section 4.2 characterizes the best predictors associated with various loss functions.

Best prediction problems are moment extremum regressions. Section 4.3 applies the method of moments to obtain analog estimates of best predictors. A by-product is the finding that a best predictor of y conditional on x solves a conceptually distinct '*ex ante*' prediction problem. Section 4.4 discusses *ex ante* prediction.

4.1 Best predictors

Let $x(*)$ be a given function mapping the sample space Z into a space X. Let a realization of the random variable z be drawn but not observed. Only the realization of $x(z)$ is observed.

Let $y(*)$ be a given function mapping Z into the real line. Suppose that one is required to make a point prediction of the unobserved realization of $y(z)$. If θ is the prediction, one suffers a random loss $L(y - \theta)$, where $L(*)$ is a specified loss function. That is, $L(*)$ maps the real line into the non-negative half-line and

$$0 < u < v \Rightarrow 0 = L(0) \leqslant L(u) \leqslant L(v)$$
$$0 = L(0) \leqslant L(-u) \leqslant L(-v) \qquad (4.1)$$

Let $b(*)$ be a function mapping X into the real line that solves the collection of problems

$$b(\xi) - \operatorname*{argmin}_{\theta \in R^1} \int L(y - \theta)\, dP_y | \xi = 0, \qquad \xi \in X \qquad (4.2)$$

That is, for each ξ in X, $b(\xi)$ minimizes on R^1 the expectation of the random loss function conditional on the event $[x = \xi]$. The function $b(*)$ is termed a best predictor of y conditional on x.

4.1.1 *Location functions*

It is appealing to think of a best predictor as a summary measure characterizing the location of y conditional on x. This idea may be given formal expression.

Let Π^0 denote the space of all probability measures on the real line. Let $l(*)$ be a function mapping Π^0 into the real line. Given any measure Q in Π^0, let $\delta(Q)$ be a random variable distributed Q. Given any real number η, let D_η be the probability measure placing all its mass on η. Let $Q \oplus D_\eta$ denote the probability measure of $\delta(Q) + \eta$. Then $l(*)$ is said to be a location function if for all Q in Π^0 and η in R^1,

$$l(Q) \oplus (D_\eta) = l(Q) + \eta \qquad (4.3)$$

A best predictor $b(*)$ is a location function evaluated at the collection of probability measures $P_y | \xi, \xi \in X$. To see this, fix ξ and let η be any real number. Suppose that instead of predicting the realization of the random variable y, one is required to predict the realization of $y + \eta$. Observe that

$$L[(y + \eta) - (\theta + \eta)] = L(y - \theta) \qquad (4.4)$$

It follows from this and from (4.2) that if $b(\xi)$ is a best predictor of y conditional on the event $[x = \xi]$, then $b(\xi) + \eta$ is a best predictor of $y + \eta$.

4.1.2 *Estimation of best predictors*

Much of the interest in the estimation of best predictors derives from the fact that best predictors are location functions. One often would like to summarize succinctly the manner in which the mass of the probability measure $P_y|\xi$ varies with ξ. Location functions do just this. Location functions that solve best prediction problems are easily interpreted. Being moment regressions, best predictor location functions are readily estimated.

Interest in the estimation of best predictors may, of course, be motivated by a need to make a real prediction. In this case, it is important to recognize that the problem of making a best prediction given sample data is not the same as that of estimating a best predictor. The former question asks how one should predict y conditional on x when the best predictor $b(*)$ is not known but a sample of observations of (y, x) is available. The latter, which is the focus of this chapter, asks how one might estimate $b(*)$ itself.

To accomplish the former objective, a possible approach is to address the latter question; that is, to estimate $b(*)$ and use the estimate $B_N(*)$ to predict y. This makes sense if $B_N(*)$ is consistent and if a large sample of observations of (y, x) is available. Then $B_N(*)$ is likely a good predictor of y, in the sense of yielding close to minimal expected loss. One cannot, however, claim that using an estimate of the best predictor to predict y offers an optimal solution to the problem of best prediction given sample data.

In fact, the literature on statistical decision theory does not present a consensus prescription for prediction when $b(*)$ is unknown but sample data are available. There is a longstanding debate between the Bayesian and frequentist schools of thought, as well as sub-debates within each school.

4.1.3 More general prediction problems

We have assumed that the random variable y is real valued and that the loss associated with using θ to predict y is a function of the difference $y - \theta$. It is possible to define conditional prediction in far more general terms.

One may let $y(*)$ be a mapping from Z into some space Y and let the loss function be a mapping from $Y \times Y$ into the non-negative half-line. Then a best predictor of y conditional on x solves

$$b(\xi) - \operatorname*{argmin}_{\theta \in Y} \int L(y, \theta)\, \mathrm{d}P_y|\xi = 0, \qquad \xi \in X \qquad (4.5)$$

Such abstract prediction problems are examined in Ferguson (1967) and Lehmann (1983). They will not be considered here.

4.2 Best predictors under various loss functions

In general, a best predictor of y conditional on x depends on the specified loss function. Two loss functions have dominated the literature. These are square loss and absolute loss.

4.2.1 *Square loss*

Let $L(*)$ be the square loss function

$$L(u) \equiv u^2 \tag{4.6}$$

Then a best predictor solves the collection of problems

$$b(\xi) - \operatorname*{argmin}_{\theta \in R^1} \int (y - \theta)^2 \, dP_y | \xi = 0, \qquad \xi \in X \tag{4.7}$$

The mean regression of y on x is the one function solving (4.7). Thus,

$$b(\xi) = \int y \, dP_y | \xi, \qquad \xi \in X \tag{4.8}$$

To establish this well-known result, fix ξ and abbreviate the notation by letting $v \equiv P_y | \xi$. Let μ denote the mean of v and let θ be any real number distinct from μ. Then

$$\int (y - \theta)^2 \, dv = \int [(y - \mu) + (\mu - \theta)]^2 \, dv$$

$$= \int (y - \mu)^2 \, dv + (\mu - \theta)^2 + 2(\mu - \theta) \left[\int (y - \mu) \, dv \right]$$

$$= \int (y - \mu)^2 \, dv + (\mu - \theta)^2$$

$$> \int (y - \mu)^2 \, dv \tag{4.9}$$

4.2.2 *Absolute loss*

Let $L(*)$ be the absolute loss function

$$L(u) \equiv |u| \tag{4.10}$$

Then a best predictor solves the problem

$$b(\xi) - \operatorname*{argmin}_{\theta \in R^1} \int |y - \theta| \, dP_y|\xi = 0, \qquad \xi \in X \qquad (4.11)$$

The median regression of y on x solves (4.11). To show this, again fix ξ and let $v \equiv P_y|\xi$. By definition, the median of v is the real number

$$m \equiv \min \theta : v(-\infty, \theta] \geqslant 1/2 \qquad (4.12)$$

where $v(-\infty, \theta]$ is the v-probability that y is in the interval $(-\infty, \theta]$.

To prove that the median is a best predictor under absolute loss, compare the expected loss at m with that at any $\theta < m$. We find

$$\int |y - \theta| \, dv - \int |y - m| \, dv = \int [|y - \theta| - |y - m|] \, dv$$

$$= \int_{(-\infty, \theta]} (\theta - m) \, dv + \int_{(\theta, m)} [2y - (\theta + m)] \, dv + \int_{[m, \infty)} (m - \theta) \, dv$$

$$\geqslant (\theta - m)v(-\infty, \theta] + (\theta - m)v(\theta, m) + (m - \theta)v[m, \infty)$$

$$= -(m - \theta)v(-\infty, m) + (m - \theta)v[m, \infty)$$

$$= (m - \theta)\{v[m, \infty) - v(-\infty, m)\} \qquad (4.13)$$

By definition (4.12) of the median, $v(-\infty, \theta] < 1/2$ for all $\theta < m$. Hence, $v(-\infty, m) \leqslant 1/2$. So the final expression in (4.13) is non-negative.

Now compare the expected loss at m with that at any $\theta > m$.

$$\int |y - \theta| \, dv - \int |y - m| \, dv = \int [|y - \theta| - |y - m|] \, dv$$

$$= \int_{(-\infty, m]} (\theta - m) \, dv + \int_{(m, \theta)} [(\theta + m) - 2y] \, dv + \int_{[\theta, \infty)} (m - \theta) \, dv$$

$$\geqslant (\theta - m)v(-\infty, m] + (m - \theta)v(m, \theta) + (m - \theta)v[\theta, \infty)$$

$$= (\theta - m)v(-\infty, m] - (\theta - m)v(m, \infty)$$

$$= (\theta - m)\{v(-\infty, m] - v(m, \infty)\} \qquad (4.14)$$

By (4.12), $v(\theta, \infty) \leqslant 1/2$ for all $\theta > m$. Hence, $v(m, \infty) \leqslant 1/2$. So the final expression in (4.14) is non-negative.

4.2.3 Mean vs. median regression

The mean and median regressions of y on x both express the central tendency of y conditional on x. It is important to recognize that these two regression functions generally do not coincide. For example, one might be a linear function of x and the other not. Or both might be linear but with different slope parameters. It is even possible that one regression function increases with x while the other decreases. A simple example suffices to show this.

Let x be a Bernoulli random variable. That is, let there be a subset Z_0 of the sample space Z such that $x(z) = 0$ for z in Z_0 and $x(z) = 1$ for z in $Z - Z_0$. Then the mean and median regressions of y on x can be written as the linear functions

$$E(y|\xi) = E(y|\xi = 0) + [E(y|\xi = 1) - E(y|\xi = 0)]\xi, \qquad \xi = 0, 1$$
$$(4.15)$$

and

$$m(y|\xi) = m(y|\xi = 0) + [m(y|\xi = 1) - m(y|\xi = 0)]\xi, \qquad \xi = 0, 1$$
$$(4.16)$$

where $E(y|\xi)$ and $m(y|\xi)$ denote the mean and median of y conditional on the event $[x = \xi]$. The slope parameters of the two regression functions are $[E(y|\xi = 1) - E(y|\xi = 0)]$ and $[m(y|\xi = 1) - m(y|\xi = 0)]$. These differences of means and medians need not be equal nor even have the same sign.

Thus, prediction of y under square and absolute loss can yield different qualitative conclusions about the central tendency of y as a function of x. The need for care in specification of a loss function disappears only if one somehow knows that the mean and median regressions of y on x coincide in the application of interest. It is often difficult to justify such knowledge. It is sometimes plausible that the probability measures $P_y|\xi$, $\xi \in X$ all have symmetric distribution functions. If so, the mean and median regressions do coincide.

4.2.4 *Asymmetric absolute loss*

The square and the absolute loss functions are both symmetric around zero. That is, they satisfy the condition

$$L(-u) = L(u), \qquad u \in R^1 \qquad (4.17)$$

Sometimes one prefers to treat over- and under-predictions asymmetrically. Among asymmetric loss functions, we shall discuss only asymmetric absolute loss. Let α be a specified constant in the interval $(0, 1)$. The α-absolute loss function is

$$L(u) = (1 - \alpha)|u| \times 1[u < 0] + \alpha|u| \times 1[u > 0] \qquad (4.18)$$

Here 1[*] denotes the function that takes the value one if the logical condition inside the brackets is satisfied and zero otherwise.

We have shown that the median regression of y on x is a best predictor under 0.5-absolute loss. This result generalizes. The α-quantile regression of y on x is a best predictor under α-absolute loss. By definition, the α-quantile of a probability measure v is the real number

$$q_\alpha \equiv \min \theta: v(-\infty, \theta] \geqslant \alpha \qquad (4.19)$$

To prove that the α-quantile is a best predictor under α-absolute loss, we generalize the argument of (4.13) and (4.14). Compare the expected loss at q_α with that at any $\theta < q_\alpha$. For $L(*)$ given in (4.18),

$$\int L(y-\theta)\,dv - \int L(y-q_\alpha)\,dv = \int [L(y-\theta) - L(y-q_\alpha)]\,dv$$

$$= (1-\alpha)\int_{(-\infty,\theta]} (\theta - q_\alpha)\,dv + \int_{(\theta,q_\alpha)} [y - \{\alpha\theta + (1-\alpha)q_\alpha\}]\,dv$$

$$+ \alpha \int_{[q_\alpha,\infty)} (q_\alpha - \theta)\,dv$$

$$\geqslant (1-\alpha)(\theta - q_\alpha)v(-\infty,\theta] + (1-\alpha)(\theta - q_\alpha)v(\theta,q_\alpha)$$

$$+ \alpha(q_\alpha - \theta)v[q_\alpha,\infty)$$

$$= -(1-\alpha)(q_\alpha - \theta)v(-\infty,q_\alpha) + \alpha(q_\alpha - \theta)v[q_\alpha,\infty)$$

$$= (q_\alpha - \theta)\{\alpha v[q_\alpha,\infty) - (1-\alpha)v(-\infty,q_\alpha)\} \qquad (4.20)$$

By (4.19), $v(-\infty,\theta] < \alpha$ for all $\theta < q_\alpha$. Hence, $v(-\infty,q_\alpha) \leqslant \alpha$. So the final expression in (4.20) is non-negative.

Now compare the expected loss at q_α with that at any $\theta > q_\alpha$.

$$\int L(y-\theta)\,dv - \int L(y-q_\alpha)\,dv = \int [L(y-\theta) - L(y-q_\alpha)]\,dv$$

$$= (1-\alpha)\int_{(-\infty,q_\alpha]} (\theta - q_\alpha)\,dv + \int_{(q_\alpha,\theta)} [\{(1-\alpha)\theta + \alpha q_\alpha\} - y]\,dv$$

$$+ \alpha \int_{[\theta,\infty)} (q_\alpha - \theta)\,dv$$

$$\geqslant (1-\alpha)(\theta - q_\alpha)v(-\infty,q_\alpha] + \alpha(q_\alpha - \theta)v(q_\alpha,\theta) + \alpha(q_\alpha - \theta)v[\theta,\infty)$$

$$= (1-\alpha)(\theta - q_\alpha)v(-\infty,q_\alpha] - \alpha(\theta - q_\alpha)v(q_\alpha,\infty)$$

$$= (\theta - q_\alpha)\{(1-\alpha)v(-\infty,q_\alpha] - \alpha v(q_\alpha,\infty)\} \qquad (4.21)$$

By (4.19), $v(\theta, \infty) \leqslant 1 - \alpha$ for all $\theta > q_\alpha$. Hence, $v(q_\alpha, \infty) \leqslant 1 - \alpha$. So the final expression in (4.21) is non-negative.

It is of interest to compare the best predictors of y under α-absolute loss as α varies. As α increases, the loss function penalizes under-predictions of y more heavily and over-predictions less heavily. The result is that a higher quantile regression becomes the best predictor.

Let $0 < \alpha_1 < \alpha_2 < 1$. For any probability measure v,

$$\alpha_1 < \alpha_2 \Rightarrow q_{\alpha_1} \leqslant q_{\alpha_2} \tag{4.22}$$

It follows that the α_2-quantile regression of y on x lies everywhere on or above the α_1-quantile regression. These two quantile regressions need not, however, be parallel. In fact, one may be increasing in x where the other is decreasing. Thus, prediction of y under the α_1- and α_2-absolute loss functions can yield different qualitative conclusions about the location of y as a function of x.

4.2.5 Translation families

The quantile regressions of y on x are parallel to one another if the conditional probability measures $P_y | \xi$, $\xi \in X$ are a 'translation family'. Assume there is a function $\eta(*)$ mapping X into the real line such that, for each ξ in X, $P_y | \xi$ is the measure of the random variable $y + \eta(\xi)$. Then $P_y | \xi$ is the same as P_y up to location. We say that $P_y | \xi$, $\xi \in X$ are a translation family.

Let $l_1(*)$ and $l_2(*)$ be any two location functions. The definition of a location function implies that for all ξ in X,

$$l_2(P_y | \xi) - l_1(P_y | \xi) = [l_2(P_y) + \eta(\xi)] - [l_1(P_y) + \eta(\xi)]$$
$$= l_2(P_y) - l_1(P_y) \tag{4.23}$$

Thus, considered as functions on X, $l_1(*)$ and $l_2(*)$ are parallel.

4.2.6 Best predictors of binary response

To conclude this discussion of loss functions, we briefly examine prediction under square and absolute loss in the special case of binary response. In binary response problems, the distribution of y conditional on the event $[x = \xi]$ is Bernoulli with unknown parameter p_ξ. That is, $y = 1$ with probability p_ξ and $y = 0$ otherwise. Binary response offers the simplest non-trivial setting for conditional prediction.

Fix ξ. The mean of y conditional on $[x = \xi]$ is

$$E(y|\xi) = p_\xi \qquad (4.24)$$

So the best predictor under square loss is p_ξ. The α-quantile of y conditional on $[x = \xi]$ is

$$q_\alpha(y|\xi) = 1[p_\xi > 1 - \alpha] \qquad (4.25)$$

Hence, under α-absolute loss, $1[p_\xi > 1 - \alpha]$ is a best predictor.

Note that for all ξ such that $p_\xi \neq 1 - \alpha$, the α-quantile $1[p_\xi > 1 - \alpha]$ is the unique best predictor under α-absolute loss. For ξ such that $p_\xi = 1 - \alpha$, on the other hand, all predictors in the interval $[0, 1]$ have the same expected loss and so are best predictors.

4.3 Method of moments estimation of best predictors

Consider the problem of estimating a best predictor $b(*)$. Thus, let a conditional prediction problem be specified. Let a random sample from P be drawn and the empirical measure P_N observed. Let it be known that $b(*)$ is in a given space B of functions mapping X into the real line.

The method of moments is the dominant approach to estimation. In Section 3.3, we obtained method of moments estimates for general moment extremum regressions. Applying those results here, let $w(*)$ be any function mapping X into the real line, with $w(\xi) > 0$ a.e. P_x. Then the problem

$$b(\xi) - \underset{\theta \in R^1}{\text{argmin}} \int L(y - \theta) dP_y | \xi = 0, \qquad \text{a.e. } P_x \qquad (4.26)$$

implies that $b(*)$ solves

$$b(*) - \underset{c \in B}{\text{argmin}} \int w\{x(z)\} L[y(z) - c\{x(z)\}] dP = 0 \qquad (4.27)$$

Application of the analogy principle to (4.27) yields a method of moments estimate, namely

$$B_N = \underset{c \in B}{\text{argmin}} \int w\{x(z)\} L[y(z) - c\{x(z)\}] dP_N \qquad (4.28)$$

Two especially prominent examples are the estimates obtained under square and absolute loss, with $w(\xi) = 1$ for all ξ. These are the least squares and least absolute deviations estimates

$$B_N = \underset{c \in B}{\operatorname{argmin}} \int [y(z) - c\{x(z)\}]^2 dP_N$$

$$= \underset{c \in B}{\operatorname{argmin}} \frac{1}{N} \sum_{i=1}^{N} [y_i - c(x_i)]^2 \tag{4.29}$$

and

$$B_N = \underset{c \in B}{\operatorname{argmin}} \int |y(z) - c\{x(z)\}| dP_N$$

$$= \underset{c \in B}{\operatorname{argmin}} \frac{1}{N} \sum_{i=1}^{N} |y_i - c(x_i)| \tag{4.30}$$

Method of moments estimation under α-absolute loss has been studied by Koenker and Bassett (1978).

4.3.1 *The parameter space*

In Chapter 3, we indicated that method of moments estimation of regression functions works well when the parameter space is sufficiently small but breaks down when it is too large. The cautionary remarks made there obviously apply here. In fact, method of moments estimation of best predictors breaks down in a particularly drastic way.

Consider the common setting in which the empirical support of x, that is $X_N \equiv (x_i, i = 1, \ldots, N)$, contains N distinct points. Let B restrict $b(*)$ only locally. Then the method of moments estimate of $b(*)$ is

$$B_N(x_i) = y_i, \qquad i = 1, \ldots, N \tag{4.31a}$$
$$B_N(\xi) = R^1, \qquad \xi \in X - X_N \tag{4.31b}$$

This holds for all loss functions and weighting functions.

It is important to understand that the failure of the method of moments when B restricts $b(*)$ only locally does not imply that consistent estimation is impossible. The nonparametric estimation methods described in Sections 3.4 and 3.5 remain available.

4.3.2 *Method of moments estimation of mean regressions*

The method of moments estimate (4.28) is well defined for any loss function. For square loss, alternative method of moments estimates exist.

Under square loss, the best predictor of y conditional on x is the mean regression of y on x. So the collection of moment extremum problems

$$b(\xi) - \operatorname*{argmin}_{\theta \in R^1} \int (y - \theta)^2 \, dP_y | \xi = 0, \qquad \xi \in X \qquad (4.32)$$

is equivalent to the collection of moment equations

$$\int [y - b(\xi)] \, dP_y | \xi = 0, \qquad \xi \in X \qquad (4.33)$$

Let $v(*)$ be any function mapping X into a real vector space. It follows from (4.33) and from the law of iterated expectations that the mean regression solves the moment equation

$$\int v\{x(z)\} [y(z) - b\{x(z)\}] \, dP = 0 \qquad (4.34)$$

That is, the prediction error $y - b(x)$ is orthogonal to any function of x. Method of moments estimates for the mean regression may be obtained by applying the analogy principle to (4.34).

4.3.3 Method of moments estimation of quantile regressions

A variation on the foregoing method for estimating mean regressions can be used to estimate some quantile regressions. Recall that the α-quantile of a probability measure v is

$$q_\alpha \equiv \min \theta : v(-\infty, \theta] \geqslant \alpha \qquad (4.35)$$

Let v be any continuous probability measure; that is, one without mass points. Then

$$v(-\infty, q_\alpha) = 1 - v(q_\alpha, \infty) = \alpha \qquad (4.36)$$

Hence,

$$(1 - \alpha) v(-\infty, q_\alpha) - \alpha v(q_\alpha, \infty) = 0 \qquad (4.37)$$

Let δ be a random variable distributed v. Then (4.37) may be restated as the moment equation

$$\int \{(1 - \alpha) * 1[\delta < q_\alpha] - \alpha * 1[\delta > q_\alpha]\} \, dv = 0 \qquad (4.38)$$

Now consider the α-quantile regression of y on x. Assume that for each ξ in X, the probability measure $P_y|\xi$ is continuous. By (4.38), the α-quantile regression solves the collection of moment equations

$$\int \{(1-\alpha)*1[y < b(\xi)] - \alpha*1[y > b(\xi)]\} dP_y|\xi = 0, \quad \xi \in X \quad (4.39)$$

As earlier, let $v(*)$ be any function mapping X into a real vector space. It follows from (4.39) and from the law of iterated expectations that the α-quantile regression solves the moment equation

$$\int v\{x(z)\}\{(1-\alpha)*1[y(z) < b(x(z))]$$
$$- \alpha*1[y(z) > b(x(z))]\} dP = 0 \quad (4.40)$$

Method of moments estimates for the α-quantile regression may be obtained by applying the analogy principle to (4.40).

Equation (4.40) simplifies in the case of median regression. There,

$$\int v\{x(z)\} \operatorname{sgn}[y(z) - b(x(z))] dP = 0 \quad (4.41)$$

where $\operatorname{sgn}(*)$ denotes the sign function. That is, $u < 0 \Leftrightarrow \operatorname{sgn}(u) = -1$; $\operatorname{sgn}(0) = 0$; and $u > 0 \Leftrightarrow \operatorname{sgn}(u) = 1$. Thus, the best predictor under symmetric absolute loss makes the sign of the prediction error $y - b(x)$ orthogonal to any function of x, provided that the measures $P_y|\xi$, $\xi \in X$ are continuous.

4.4   *Ex ante* prediction

By definition, a best predictor of y conditional on x solves

$$b(\xi) - \operatorname*{argmin}_{\theta \in R^1} \int L(y - \theta) dP_y|\xi = 0, \qquad \xi \in X \quad (4.42)$$

By the law of iterated expectations, a best predictor solves

$$b(*) - \operatorname*{argmin}_{c \in B} \int L[y(z) - c\{x(z)\}] dP = 0 \quad (4.43)$$

provided that the space B of predictor functions contains a solution to (4.42). In the preceding section, we used (4.43) and weighted versions thereof to obtain method of moments estimates for best predictors. Here we call attention to the fact that (4.43) is itself a prediction problem.

Problems (4.42) and (4.43) are conceptually distinct. In (4.42), a realization of (y, x) has been drawn and the event $[x = \xi]$ has been observed. The problem is to minimize over θ in R^1 the expectation of $L(y - \theta)$ with respect to the measure $P_y|\xi$. In (4.43), a realization of (y, x) will be drawn and the realization of x then observed. Before this occurs, a predictor function must be chosen. The problem is to minimize over $c(*)$ in B the expectation of $L[y(z) - c\{x(z)\}]$ with respect to the measure P.

The same function $b(*)$ solves both the *ex post* prediction problem (4.42) and the *ex ante* problem (4.43). This fact is a simple but remarkable consequence of the linearity of the expectation operator.

4.4.1 *Best linear predictors*

Consider the space B of predictor functions appearing in (4.43). Thus far, we have assumed that B contains a solution to (4.42). Now drop this assumption and permit B to be any space of functions mapping X into the real line. Then problem (4.43) remains well defined, but is no longer equivalent to problem (4.42).

By far the most extensively studied *ex ante* prediction problem is that in which X is K-dimensional real space and B is the space of all linear functions mapping R^K into the real line. That is,

$$B \equiv [(\xi'\gamma, \xi \in X), \gamma \in R^K] \qquad (4.44)$$

where ξ' is the transpose of the column vector ξ. With this specification of B, a function solving (4.43) is termed a best linear predictor. The analog estimate of a best linear predictor is

$$B_N \equiv [(\xi'\gamma, \xi \in X), \gamma \in \Gamma_N] \qquad (4.45)$$

where

$$\Gamma_N \equiv \underset{\gamma \in R^K}{\text{argmin}} \int L[y(z) - x(z)'\gamma] \, dP_N$$

$$= \underset{\gamma \in R^K}{\text{argmin}} \frac{1}{N} \sum_{i=1}^{N} L(y_i - x_i'\gamma) \qquad (4.46)$$

Best linear predictors are sometimes called linear regressions. We shall not use this phrase. As defined in Chapter 3, a regression is a function $b(*)$ with domain X such that for each ξ in X, the value $b(\xi)$ depends on P only through the conditional measure $P|\xi$. Best linear predictors have this property only if a linear function solves problem

(4.42). Otherwise, a solution to problem (4.43) must trade off lower expected loss for predictions at some realizations of x against higher expected loss for predictions at others. The optimal tradeoff depends on the set of conditional measures $P|\xi$, $\xi \in X$ and on the marginal measure P_x as well.

It is worth noting that a best linear predictor does solve problem (4.42) if the space X is sufficiently small. Assume that X contains L points. Let $b(*)$ solve problem (4.42). If $L \leq K$, then there always exists a γ in R^K that solves the set of L linear equations $b(\xi) = \xi'\gamma$, $\xi \in X$. (In Section 4.2, we used this fact to write the mean and median regressions of y on a Bernoulli random variable x as linear functions.)

CHAPTER 5

Conditional likelihood problems

Recall the definition of a likelihood problem given in Chapter 2. Probability measure P on the sample space Z is known to be absolutely continuous with respect to a given measure v on Z. That is,

$$v(A) = 0 \Rightarrow P(A) = 0, \qquad A \subset Z \qquad (5.1)$$

A given function $\tau(*)$ maps each element of the parameter space B into a probability measure on Z. The measures $[\tau(c), c \in B]$ are all absolutely continuous with respect to v. The parameter b solves the index problem

$$P - \tau(b) = 0 \qquad (5.2)$$

In Chapter 2 we stated that, in the context of (5.1), b solves (5.2) if and only if b also solves the moment problem

$$b - \underset{c \in B}{\text{argmax}} \int \log \varphi_v[z, \tau(c)] \, dP = 0 \qquad (5.3)$$

where $\varphi_v[*, \tau(c)]$ is the density of $\tau(c)$ with respect to v. This fact, which underlies maximum likelihood estimation, will be proved here.

Actually, we shall consider a regression version of the likelihood problem. It is rare in econometric work to assume that a parameter of interest indexes the probability measure of the entire observable random vector. It is relatively common, on the other hand, to assume that a parameter indexes a collection of conditional probability measures.

5.1 The estimation problem

Let $y(*)$ and $x(*)$ be given functions mapping Z into spaces Y and X

respectively. Let it be known that for each ξ in X, the conditional probability measure $P_y|\xi$ is absolutely continuous with respect to a given measure v_ξ on Y. Thus,

$$v_\xi(A) = 0 \Rightarrow P_y(A|\xi) = 0, \qquad A \subset Y \tag{5.4}$$

Henceforth, we say that v_ξ dominates $P_y|\xi$. In applications, the dominating measures $v_\xi, \xi \in X$ usually coincide. We shall nevertheless allow for the possibility that v_ξ varies with ξ.

Let Θ be a given space. Let $[\tau_\xi(\theta), \theta \in \Theta]$ be a given family of probability measures on Y, all dominated by v_ξ. Let the parameter space B be a space of functions mapping X into Θ. Let it be known that $b(*)$ solves the collection of index problems

$$P_y|\xi - \tau_\xi[b(\xi)] = 0, \qquad \xi \in X \tag{5.5}$$

5.1.1 The likelihood inequality

In the context of (5.4), $b(*)$ solves (5.5) if and only if $b(*)$ also solves the collection of moment problems

$$b(\xi) - \underset{\theta \in \Theta}{\mathrm{argmax}} \int \log \varphi_\xi(y, \theta) \, \mathrm{d}P_y|\xi = 0, \qquad \xi \in X \tag{5.6}$$

Here $\varphi_\xi(*, \theta)$, an abbreviated notation for $\varphi_\xi[*, \tau_\xi(\theta)]$, is the density of $\tau_\xi(\theta)$ with respect to v_ξ. That is, $\varphi_\xi(*, \theta)$ is a non-negative valued function on Y such that

$$\tau_\xi(\theta)(A) = \int_A \varphi_\xi(y, \theta) \, \mathrm{d}v_\xi, \qquad A \subset Y \tag{5.7}$$

The key tool used to show the equivalence of (5.5) and (5.6) is Jensen's inequality:

Let Q be a probability measure on Y. Let $h(*)$ be a function mapping Y into the real line. Let $f(*)$ be a concave function on the real line. Then $\int f[h(y)] \, \mathrm{d}Q \leqslant f[\int h(y) \mathrm{d}Q]$. Let $f(*)$ be strictly concave. Then $\int f[h(y)] \, \mathrm{d}Q = f[\int h(y) \mathrm{d}Q]$ if and only if $h(*)$ is constant a.e. Q.

For a proof, see Lehmann (1983) or Rao (1973).

Fix ξ and consider θ in Θ. The function $\log(*)$ is strictly concave.

Hence, by Jensen's inequality,

$$\int \log \varphi_\xi(y, \theta) \, dP_y|\xi - \int \log \varphi_\xi[y, b(\xi)] \, dP_y|\xi$$

$$= \int \log \frac{\varphi_\xi(y, \theta)}{\varphi_\xi[y, b(\xi)]} \, dP_y|\xi$$

$$\leqslant \log \int \frac{\varphi_\xi(y, \theta)}{\varphi_\xi[y, b(\xi)]} \, dP_y|\xi \qquad (5.8)$$

By the absolute continuity of $P_y|\xi$,

$$\log \int \frac{\varphi_\xi(y, \theta)}{\varphi_\xi[y, b(\xi)]} \, dP_y|\xi$$

$$= \log \int \frac{\varphi_\xi(y, \theta)}{\varphi_\xi[y, b(\xi)]} \, \varphi_\xi[y, b(\xi)] \, dv_\xi$$

$$= \log \left[\int \varphi_\xi(y, \theta) \, dv_\xi \right]$$

$$= 0 \qquad (5.9)$$

So (5.5) implies (5.6).

The weak inequality (5.8) is an equality if and only if $\varphi_\xi(y, \theta) = \varphi_\xi[y, b(\xi)]$ a.e. $P_y|\xi$. These densities agree almost everywhere if and only if the probability measures $\tau_\xi(\theta)$ and $\tau_\xi[b(\xi)]$ coincide. So (5.6) implies (5.5).

5.1.2 *Identification*

The above suggests that $b(*)$ is identified if, for each $c(*) \neq b(*)$, there exists a ξ in X such that $\tau_\xi[c(\xi)] \neq P_y|\xi$. Recall, however, that any regression problem is indeterminate up to sets of P_x-measure zero. Hence, (5.5) and (5.6) are really the same as

$$P_y|\xi - \tau_\xi[b(\xi)] = 0, \qquad \text{a.e. } P_x \qquad (5.10)$$

and

$$b(\xi) - \underset{\theta \in \Theta}{\operatorname{argmax}} \int \log \varphi_\xi(y, \theta) \, dP_y|\xi = 0, \qquad \text{a.e. } P_x \qquad (5.11)$$

With this modification, a meaningful identification statement can be made. For c in B, let

$$X_c \equiv [\xi \in X : \tau_\xi\{c(\xi)\} \neq P_y|\xi] \qquad (5.12)$$

Then $b(*)$ is identified if and only if $P_x(X_c) > 0$ for every $c(*) \neq b(*)$.

5.1.3 *Dominating measures*

Definition of a conditional likelihood problem presumes that for each ξ in X, one can specify a measure which dominates the probability measure $P_y|\xi$. When the space Y is countable, this requirement is innocuous. Let v_ξ be counting measure, that is the measure which assigns mass one to each element of Y. Then every non-empty subset of Y has positive mass under v_ξ. So (5.4) imposes no restrictions on $P_y|\xi$.

When Y is an uncountable set, specifying a dominating measure generally implies some knowledge of $P_y|\xi$. That is, certain non-empty subsets of Y are known to have probability zero. To make the point, it suffices to consider the case in which Y is the real line. In particular, let us contrast three classes of problems, each prominent in applications.

In a 'continuous' problem, it is known that $P_y|\xi$ is dominated by Lebesgue measure μ. Lebesgue measure assigns to each interval on R^1 a mass equal to its length. Dominance by μ implies that all countable and some uncountable subsets of R^1 have probability zero under $P_y|\xi$.

In a 'discrete' problem, it is known that $P_y|\xi$ is dominated by a given discrete measure, denoted D. Measure D places positive mass on each element of some countable set Y_D of the line and assigns zero mass elsewhere. (The set Y_D may be finite. Binary response is the case in which Y_D has two elements.) Dominance by D implies that every subset of R^1 whose intersection with Y_D is null has probability zero under $P_y|\xi$.

In a 'mixed' problem, it is known that $P_y|\xi$ is dominated by the sum of Lebesgue measure μ and a given discrete measure D. Let $v \equiv \mu + D$. Dominance by v implies that every subset of R^1 which has both μ-measure zero and D-measure zero has probability zero under $P_y|\xi$.

Censoring generates a simple, empirically important example of a mixed problem. Let $h(*)$ be a function mapping Z into the real line. Let it be known that $P_h|\xi$ is dominated by Lebesgue measure. For ζ in Z, let $y(\zeta) \equiv \max[0, h(\zeta)]$. Then $P_y|\xi$ is dominated neither by Lebesgue measure nor by any discrete measure. But $P_y|\xi$ is dominated by the sum of Lebesgue measure and the discrete measure placing all its mass on the point set $\{0\}$.

5.2 Maximum likelihood estimation

To obtain an estimator for $b(*)$, we may apply the results of Section 3.3. By the law of iterated expectations, the collection of moment problems

$$b(\xi) - \operatorname*{argmax}_{\theta \in \Theta} \int \log \varphi_\xi(y, \theta) \, dP_y | \xi = 0, \qquad \text{a.e. } P_x \qquad (5.13)$$

is equivalent to the moment problem

$$b(*) - \operatorname*{argmax}_{c \in B} \int \log \left[\varphi_{x(z)}[y(z), c\{x(z)\}] \right] dP = 0 \qquad (5.14)$$

Application of the analogy principle to (5.14) yields the maximum likelihood estimate

$$B_N \equiv \operatorname*{argmax}_{c \in B} \int \log \left[\varphi_{x(z)}[y(z), c\{x(z)\}] \right] dP_N$$

$$= \operatorname*{argmax}_{c \in B} \frac{1}{N} \sum_{i=1}^N \log \varphi_{x_i}[y_i, c(x_i)] \qquad (5.15)$$

Note that maximum likelihood estimation is well defined whether or not, for $\xi \in (x_i, i = 1, \ldots, N)$, the conditional empirical measure $P_{Ny} | \xi$ is dominated by v_ξ.

Maximum likelihood estimation is one among many analog methods for estimation of a parameter solving a likelihood problem. Other approaches include the classical method of moments and minimum distance estimation, discussed in Sections 2.1 and 2.4. Relative to alternative procedures, maximum likelihood estimation is distinguished by its asymptotic efficiency, at least in suitably regular problems. This topic will be covered in Section 8.4.

5.3 Likelihood representation of prediction problems

Specifying a conditional likelihood problem ordinarily presumes belief in the specification. For each ξ in X, one knows that v_ξ dominates $P_y | \xi$. Moreover, one knows that $P_y | \xi$ is a member of the family $[\tau_\xi(\theta), \theta \in \Theta]$.

Applied to a misspecified problem, maximum likelihood estimation often lacks a natural interpretation. All that can be said is that the parameter being estimated is the statistical function

$$b(*) \equiv \underset{c \in B}{\mathrm{argmax}} \int \log \left[\varphi_{x(z)}[y(z), c\{x(z)\}] \right] dP \qquad (5.16)$$

Some conditional likelihood problems, however, are interpretable even if aspects of the specification are incorrect. A leading case is the class of problems having a conditional prediction interpretation.

Let Y be the real line. Let $L(*)$ be a specified loss function. Let $b(*)$ be a best predictor of y conditional on x. Thus, $b(*)$ solves the collection of problems

$$b(\xi) - \underset{\theta \in R^1}{\mathrm{argmin}} \int L(y - \theta) \, dP_y | \xi = 0, \qquad \xi \in X \qquad (5.17)$$

Let ρ and κ be any positive numbers. Then for all ξ,

$$\underset{\theta \in R^1}{\mathrm{argmin}} \int L(y - \theta) \, dP_y | \xi$$

$$= \underset{\theta \in R^1}{\mathrm{argmax}} - \rho \int L(y - \theta) \, dP_y | \xi + \log(\kappa)$$

$$= \underset{\theta \in R^1}{\mathrm{argmax}} \int \log \left[\kappa * \exp\left[- \rho L(y - \theta) \right] \right] dP_y | \xi \qquad (5.18)$$

So (5.17) is equivalent to the collection of problems

$$b(\xi) - \underset{\theta \in R^1}{\mathrm{argmax}} \int \log \left[\kappa^* \exp\left[- \rho L(y - \theta) \right] \right] dP_y | \xi = 0, \quad \xi \in X$$
$$(5.19)$$

Equation (5.19) almost has the form of a conditional likelihood problem. The only flaw is that the integrals $\int \kappa * \exp\left[- \rho L(y - \theta) \right] dv_\xi$, $\theta \in R^1$ need not equal one for arbitrary ρ, κ, v_ξ, and $L(*)$. On the other hand, these adding-up conditions may hold for particular choices of ρ, κ, v_ξ, and $L(*)$. We shall show that if $L(*)$ is sufficiently regular, the adding-up conditions are satisfied when v_ξ is chosen to be Lebesgue measure and κ is made an appropriate function of ρ.

Let $L(*)$ be any homogeneous loss function such that $\exp\left[- L(v) \right]$ is integrable with respect to Lebesgue measure μ. Homogeneity means that for some $\lambda > 0$, $\rho L(v) = L(\rho^\lambda v)$ for all real v and positive

ρ. The integrability requirement is that $\int \exp[-L(v)]\,d\mu$ be finite. For such a loss function,

$$\int \kappa * \exp[-\rho L(y-\theta)]\,d\mu = \kappa \int \exp[-\rho L(v)]\,d\mu$$

$$= \kappa \int \exp[-L(\rho^\lambda v)]\,d\mu$$

$$= \kappa \rho^{-\lambda} \int \exp[-L(v)]\,d\mu \qquad (5.20)$$

Thus, $\int \kappa * \exp[-\rho L(y-\theta)]\,d\mu$ is finite for all ρ, κ, and θ. The value of this integral varies with ρ and with κ but not with θ.

Now define

$$\kappa(\rho) \equiv \rho^\lambda \left[\int \exp\{-L(v)\}\,d\mu \right]^{-1} \qquad (5.21)$$

Then for all real θ and all positive ρ,

$$\int \kappa(\rho) \exp[-\rho L(y-\theta)]\,d\mu = 1 \qquad (5.22)$$

So $\kappa(\rho)\exp[-\rho L(y-\theta)]$ is a legitimate density with respect to Lebesgue measure. Hence,

$$b(\xi) - \operatorname*{argmax}_{\theta \in R^1} \int \log\left[\kappa(\rho) * \exp[-\rho L(y-\theta)]\right]\,dP_{y|\xi} = 0,$$
$$\xi \in X \quad (5.23)$$

which is an alternative representation of the prediction problem (5.17), has the form of a conditional likelihood problem.

5.3.1 Square and absolute loss

The square and absolute loss functions are homogeneous and satisfy the integrability requirement. Let us determine the likelihood representations of prediction under these loss functions.

Consider square loss $L(v) \equiv v^2$. Here $\rho L(v) = L(\rho^{1/2}v)$ so $\lambda = 1/2$. The value of $\int \exp(-v^2)\,d\mu$ is $\pi^{1/2}$. It follows that

$$\kappa(\rho)\exp[-\rho L(y-\theta)] = (\rho/\pi)^{1/2}\exp[-\rho(y-\theta)^2] \qquad (5.24)$$

This is the density of the normal distribution with mean θ and variance $(2\rho)^{-1}$.

Now consider absolute loss $L(v) = |v|$. Here $\rho|v| = |\rho v|$ so $\lambda = 1$. The value of $\int \exp(-|v|) \, d\mu$ is 2. Hence,

$$\kappa(\rho) \exp[-\rho L(y - \theta)] = (\rho/2) \exp(-\rho|y - \theta|) \qquad (5.25)$$

This is the density of the Laplace distribution with mean θ and variance $2/\rho^2$.

5.3.2 Interpretation of the maximum likelihood estimate

The method of moments estimate derived from the prediction problem (5.17) is

$$B_N \equiv \operatorname*{argmin}_{c \in B} \frac{1}{N} \sum_{i=1}^{N} L[y_i - c(x_i)] \qquad (5.26)$$

The maximum likelihood estimate derived from the conditional likelihood problem (5.23) is

$$B_N \equiv \operatorname*{argmax}_{c \in B} \frac{1}{N} \sum_{i=1}^{N} \log\left[\kappa(\rho) * \exp[-\rho L\{y_i - c(x_i)\}]\right]$$

$$= \operatorname*{argmax}_{c \in B} \frac{1}{N} \sum_{i=1}^{N} -\rho L[y_i - c(x_i)] + \log[\kappa(\rho)]$$

$$= \operatorname*{argmin}_{c \in B} \frac{1}{N} \sum_{i=1}^{N} L[y_i - c(x_i)] \qquad (5.27)$$

Thus, the estimates (5.26) and (5.27) are identical. Indeed, the maximum likelihood estimate for $b(*)$ remains B_N if ρ is not fixed but rather is treated as a parameter to be estimated. That is, maximization of the sample likelihood over (c, ρ) in $B \times (0, \infty)$ yields the same estimate for $b(*)$ as does maximization over c in B, with ρ fixed.

How then should one interpret the parameter estimated by B_N? Interpretation must depend on one's state of knowledge. One may know that, for some positive ρ and for each ξ in X, $P_y|\xi$ is dominated by Lebesgue measure and has density in the family $\kappa(\rho) \exp[-\rho L(y - \theta)]$, $\theta \in R^1$. If so, B_N may be interpreted as estimating a parameter that indexes $P_y|\xi$, $\xi \in X$. This parameter is also the best predictor of y under $L(*)$.

One may know only that the space B contains a best predictor of y

under $L(*)$. If so, B_N may be interpreted as estimating a best predictor. This best predictor cannot, however, be said to index $P_y|\xi$, $\xi \in X$.

It may be that one brings no knowledge. If so, B_N cannot be said to estimate a best predictor. One may only interpret B_N as estimating a best *ex ante* predictor among the set of predictor functions B.

CHAPTER 6

Moment problems implied by econometric models

Let us restate the abstract econometric model introduced in Chapter 2. A random pair (z, u) takes values in a sample space $Z \times U$. Realizations of z are observed but those of u are not. A parameter b in a specified parameter space B solves an equation

$$f(z, u, b) = 0 \qquad (6.1)$$

where $f(*, *, *)$ maps $Z \times U \times B$ into a vector space.

Equation (6.1) has no content in the absence of information on the probability measure P_{zu} generating (z, u). A meaningful model combines (6.1) with suitable distributional knowledge. The literature has emphasized knowledge of the behavior of u conditional on some function of z. Thus, let $x(*)$ map Z into a space X. For ξ in X, let $P_u | \xi$ denote the probability measure of u conditional on the event $[x(z) = \xi]$. Then a model may be defined by an equation $f(z, u, b) = 0$ and by a restriction on the collection of conditional measures $[P_u | \xi, \xi \in X]$.

Consider the problem of estimating b. Estimation by the analogy principle requires representation of the model in a form that relates b to the probability measure of z. Often, the derived representation refers to unrestricted features of $P_u | x$. These features must be estimated with b. Our focus is estimation of b; hence we shall refer to estimated features of $P_u | x$ as a nuisance parameter.

Econometric research has concentrated on models which imply that b and the nuisance parameter (if there is one) solve a moment problem. Two classes of models are especially prominent. One combines restrictions on $P_u | x$ with a function f that is separable in the unobserved variables. That is,

$$f(z, u, b) \equiv u_0(z, b) - u \qquad (6.2)$$

where $u_0(*, *)$ maps $Z \times B$ into U. The other combines restrictions on $P_u | x$ with a 'response' function specification of f. Here,

$$f(z, u, b) \equiv y(z) - y_0[x(z), u, b] \qquad (6.3)$$

$y(*)$ maps Z into a space Y, and $y_0(*, *, *)$ maps $X \times U \times B$ into Y.

Section 6.1 obtains moment problems implied by models with f separable in u. Section 6.2 generates moment problems from response models.

6.1 Models separable in the unobserved variables

Let realizations of (z, u) be related to b through an equation

$$u_0(z, b) - u = 0 \qquad (6.4)$$

In the absence of restrictions on P_{zu}, (6.4) simply defines u; it carries no information about b. Combining (6.4) with various distributional restrictions implies that b and a nuisance parameter solve a type of moment equation known as an orthogonality condition.

6.1.1 Orthogonality conditions

Let X be a real vector space. Let Γ denote a space in which a nuisance parameter γ lives. Let $e(*, *)$ be a given function mapping $U \times \Gamma$ into a real vector space. Let $e(*, *)'$ denote the transpose of the column vector $e(*, *)$. The random vectors $x(z)$ and $e(u, \gamma)$ are said to be orthogonal if

$$\int x(z) e(u, \gamma)' \, dP_{zu} = 0 \qquad (6.5)$$

Let it be known that P_{zu} satisfies (6.5). Then it follows from (6.4) that (b, γ) solves the moment equation

$$\int x(z) e[u_0(z, b), \gamma]' \, dP = 0 \qquad (6.6)$$

Equation (6.6) is an orthogonality condition.

Orthogonality conditions are not meant to be motivated directly. They are rather to be seen as the consequence of other, more interpretable distributional restrictions. Some leading cases follow.

6.1.2 Mean independence

The literature on instrumental variables is concerned with models in which x and u are known to be uncorrelated. Let γ be the mean of u. Zero covariance is the orthogonality condition

$$\int x(z)[u_0(z, b) - \gamma]'\,\mathrm{d}P = 0 \tag{6.7}$$

Most authors incorporate the nuisance parameter γ into the specification of $u_0(*, *)$ by giving that function a free intercept. This done, u is declared to have mean zero and (6.7) is rewritten as

$$\int x(z)[u_0(z, b)]'\,\mathrm{d}P = 0 \tag{6.8}$$

To facilitate discussion of a variety of distributional restrictions, we shall go against convention and leave γ explicit.

Zero covariance is sometimes asserted directly, as an expression of a belief that the random variables x and u are unrelated. It is usually preferable to think of zero covariance as following from a stronger form of unrelatedness. This is the mean-independence condition

$$\int u\,\mathrm{d}P_u|\xi = \gamma, \qquad \xi \in X \tag{6.9}$$

It is often difficult to motivate zero covariance in the absence of mean independence. To see why, rewrite (6.7) as

$$\int x(z)[u_0(z, b) - \gamma]'\,\mathrm{d}P = \int x\left[\int (u - \gamma)'\,\mathrm{d}P_u|x\right]\mathrm{d}P_x = 0 \tag{6.10}$$

This shows that mean independence implies zero covariance. It also shows that x and u are uncorrelated if positive and negative realizations of $\int (u - \gamma)'\,\mathrm{d}P_u|x$ balance when weighted by the distribution of x. But one rarely has information about P_x, certainly not information that would make one confident in (6.10) in the absence of (6.9). Hence, an assertion of zero covariance suggests a belief that x and u are unrelated in the sense of mean independence.

Mean independence implies orthogonality conditions beyond (6.7). Let $v(*)$ be any function mapping X into a real vector space. It follows from (6.4) and (6.9) that

$$\int v[x(z)][u_0(z,b)-\gamma]'\,dP = \int v(x)\left[\int (u-\gamma)'\,dP_u|x\right]dP_x = 0$$

(6.11)

provided only that the integral in (6.11) exists. So the random variables $v[x(z)]$ and $u_0(z,b)$ are uncorrelated. In other words, all functions of x are instrumental variables.

6.1.3 Median independence

The assertion that u is mean independent of x expresses a belief that u has the same central tendency conditional on each realization of x. Median independence offers another expression of such a belief. Median independence *per se* does not imply an orthogonality condition. Median independence does imply orthogonality when the conditional measures $P_u|\xi$, $\xi \in X$ are componentwise continuous.

Let U be the real line. For each ξ in X, let m_ξ be the median of u conditional on the event $[x = \xi]$. Let γ be the unconditional median of u. We say that u is median independent of x if

$$m_\xi = \gamma, \qquad \xi \in X$$

(6.12)

It was shown in Chapter 4 that if $P_u|\xi, \xi \in X$ are continuous probability measures, their medians solve the moment equations

$$\int \mathrm{sgn}\,(u - m_\xi)\,dP_u|\xi = 0, \qquad \xi \in X$$

(6.13)

So median independence and continuity imply that

$$\int \mathrm{sgn}\,(u - \gamma)\,dP_u|\xi = 0, \qquad \xi \in X$$

(6.14)

It follows from (6.4) and (6.14) that

$$\int v[x(z)]\,\mathrm{sgn}\,[u_0(z,b)-\gamma]\,dP = \int v(x)\left[\int \mathrm{sgn}\,(u-\gamma)\,dP_u|x\right]dP_x = 0$$

(6.15)

for all $v(*)$ such that the integral in (6.15) exists. Thus, all functions of x are orthogonal to $\mathrm{sgn}\,[u_0(z,b)-\gamma]$.

The above argument for real-valued u extends to models in which u

is a real vector. Let u_i denote the ith component of u and let γ_i be the median of u_i. Assume that u_i is median independent of x and continuously distributed conditional on each realization of x. Then all functions of x are orthogonal to sgn $[u_{0_i}(z,b) - \gamma_i]$.

6.1.4 Conditional symmetry

Mean and median independence both express a belief that the central tendency of u does not vary with x. Yet they are different assertions with distinct consequences for estimation of b. This fact may cause the applied researcher some unavoidable discomfort. One often feels at ease saying that the central tendency of u does not vary with x. But only occasionally can one pinpoint the mathematical sense in which the term 'central tendency' should be interpreted.

The need for care in defining central tendency disappears if the conditional measures $P_u|\xi$, $\xi \in X$ are componentwise symmetric with common center of symmetry. Assume that for all realizations of x, the conditional distribution of the ith component of u is symmetric around some point γ_i on the real line. That is,

$$P_{u_i - \gamma_i}|\xi = P_{\gamma_i - u_i}|\xi, \qquad \xi \in X \qquad (6.16)$$

Let $h(*)$ be any odd function mapping the real line into a real vector space; that is, $h(\eta) = -h(-\eta)$ for η in R^1. Conditional symmetry implies

$$\int h(u_i - \gamma_i)\,dP_{u_i}|\xi = 0, \qquad \xi \in X \qquad (6.17)$$

Equations (6.4) and (6.17) imply that (b, γ) solves

$$\int v[x(z)]h[u_{0_i}(z,b) - \gamma_i]'\,dP = \int v(x)\left[\int h(u_i - \gamma_i)'\,dP_{u_i}|x\right]dP_x = 0$$

$$(6.18)$$

for all $v(*)$ and $h(*)$ such that the integral in (6.18) exists. So all functions of x are orthogonal to all odd functions of $u_i - \gamma_i$.

The functions $h(u_i - \gamma_i) \equiv u_i - \gamma_i$ and $h(u_i - \gamma_i) \equiv \mathrm{sgn}\,(u_i - \gamma_i)$ are odd. Thus, the orthogonality conditions (6.11) and (6.15) that follow from mean and median independence are satisfied given conditional symmetry.

6.1.5 *Variance independence*

One may believe that u not only has the same central tendency for each realization of x but also the same spread. The econometrics literature has tended to express spread by variance. Variance independence (homoskedasticity) is the condition

$$\int (u - \gamma_1)(u - \gamma_1)' \, dP_u | \xi = \gamma_2, \qquad \xi \in X \qquad (6.19)$$

Here γ_1 is the common mean of the measures $P_u | \xi$, $\xi \in X$ and γ_2 is the common variance matrix.

Let $v(*)$ by any function on X. Let i and j denote any components of the random vector u. It follows from (6.4) and (6.19) that (b, γ_1, γ_2) solves the orthogonality condition

$$\int v[x(z)] * \left[[u_{0_i}(z, b) - \gamma_{1_i}][u_{0_j}(z, b) - \gamma_{1_j}] - \gamma_{2_{ij}} \right] dP = 0 \quad (6.20)$$

Note that the assertion of variance independence imposes no restrictions on the variance matrix γ_2. In some applications, information about γ_2 is available. For example, it may be known that the components of u are uncorrelated with one another. Then γ_2 is a diagonal matrix. Such information may be expressed by restricting the parameter space for the moment equation (6.20).

6.1.6 *Statistical independence*

It is sometimes known that u has the same distribution for each realization of x. That is,

$$P_u | \xi = P_u, \qquad \xi \in X \qquad (6.21)$$

Statistical independence implies mean, median, and variance independence. Moreover, it implies that all functions of x are uncorrelated with all functions of u.

Let $g(*)$ map U into a real vector space. Let γ be the unconditional mean of $g(u)$. It follows from (6.21) that

$$\int g(u) \, dP_u | \xi = \gamma, \qquad \xi \in X \qquad (6.22)$$

It follows from (6.4) and (6.22) that (b, γ) solves

$$\int v[x(z)] [g\{u_0(z, b)\} - \gamma]' \, dP = 0 \qquad (6.23)$$

for all $v(*)$ and $g(*)$ such that the integral in (6.23) exists.

6.1.7 *Method of moments estimation*

Suppose that an econometric model implies an orthogonality condition. Then one may select an origin-preserving transformation and apply the analogy principle to this moment equation. The result is a method of moments estimate for (b, γ).

Method of moments estimation of separable econometric models is readily understood and widely applicable. It is of historical interest to note that the ideas presented in this section have taken considerable time to evolve.

Wright (1928) and Reiersol (1941, 1945) developed the zero covariance condition (6.7) in the case where U is the real line, X and B are both K-dimensional real space, and $u_0(*, *)$ is linear in b. In this setting, the sample analog of the orthogonality condition generally has a solution.

For some time, the literature offered no clear prescription for estimation when the vector x is longer than b; that is, when there are more instruments than unknowns. The sample analog of the zero covariance condition then usually has no solution. The idea of selecting an estimate that makes the sample condition hold as closely as possible took hold in the 1950s, particularly following the work of Sargan (1958).

It was not until the 1970s that the estimation methods developed for linear models were extended to models that are nonlinear in b. See Amemiya (1974). And it was not until the late 1970s that systematic attention was paid to distributional restrictions other than mean independence. The work of Koenker and Bassett (1978) did much to awaken interest in models assuming median independence.

The idea that orthogonality conditions should be thought of as a special case of moment equations has taken hold only in the 1980s. See Burguete, Gallant and Souza (1982), Hansen (1982), and Manski (1983).

.

6.2 Response models

Many econometric models assert that an observable random variable y is a function of a random pair (x, u), where x is observable and u is not. The mapping from (x, u) to y is known to be a member of a family of functions indexed by a parameter b in a parameter space B. Thus, realizations of z and u are related through an equation

$$y(z) - y_0[x(z), u, b] = 0 \qquad (6.24)$$

where $y(*)$ maps Z into a real vector space Y and $y_0(*, *, *)$ maps $X \times U \times B$ into Y. Equation (6.24) is meaningful only when accompanied by suitable distributional information. The literature emphasizes restrictions on the conditional probability measures $P_u | x$.

The random variable y is referred to variously as the dependent, endogenous, explained, or response variable. The pair (x, u) are termed independent, exogenous, explanatory, or stimulus variables. $y_0(*, *, *)$ is sometimes called a response function. We shall use the term 'response model' to refer to the class of econometric models which combine an equation $y - y_0(x, u, b) = 0$ with restrictions on $P_u | x$.

6.2.1 Index problem representation of response models

Every response model can be represented as a collection of index problems. Equation (6.24) states that a realization of y is determined by the realization of x and by the unobserved pair (b, u). It follows that for each ξ in X, the conditional probability measure $P_y | \xi$ is determined by $(b, P_u | \xi)$. That is, the parameter $(b, P_u | \xi)$ indexes $P_y | \xi$.

Let us state this formally. Fix ξ. For $c \in B$ and $A \subset Y$, define

$$U(\xi, c, A) \equiv u \in U \quad \text{s.t.} \quad y_0(\xi, u, c) \in A \qquad (6.25)$$

Let the available distributional information restrict $P_u | \xi$ to a family Γ_ξ of probability measures on U. For (c, γ) in $B \times \Gamma_\xi$, let $\tau_\xi(c, \gamma)$ be the probability measure on Y defined by

$$\tau_\xi(c, \gamma)(A) \equiv \gamma[U(\xi, c, A)], \qquad A \subset Y \qquad (6.26)$$

By (6.24),

$$P_y(A | \xi) = P_u[U(\xi, b, A) | \xi], \qquad A \subset Y \qquad (6.27)$$

It follows that

$$P_y | \xi = \tau_\xi(b, P_u | \xi) \qquad (6.28)$$

Thus, $P_y|\xi$ is a member of the family of measures $[\tau_\xi(c,\gamma),\ (c,\gamma)\in B \times \Gamma_\xi]$.

6.2.2 Models implying conditional likelihood problems

The above suggests that the parameter $(b, P_u|\xi)$ may solve a likelihood problem. This is so provided that the available information implies knowledge of a measure dominating $P_y|\xi$. That is, $(b, P_u|\xi)$ solves a likelihood problem if there exists a measure v_ξ on Y such that for all (c,γ) in $B \times \Gamma_\xi$,

$$v_\xi(A) = 0 \Rightarrow \tau_\xi(c,\gamma)(A) = 0, \qquad A \subset Y \qquad (6.29)$$

If (6.29) holds for each ξ in X, $[b, (P_u|\xi, \xi\in X)]$ solves a conditional likelihood problem.

Two simple special cases are prominent in applications. In discrete response models, the space Y in which y and $y_0(*, *, *)$ live is countable. So condition (6.29) is satisfied trivially by letting v_ξ be counting measure on Y. All discrete response models have conditional likelihood representations.

In separable response models, Y is a finite-dimensional real space, $U = Y$, and (6.24) has the form

$$y(z) - g[x(z), b] - u = 0 \qquad (6.30)$$

where $g(*, *)$ is a given function mapping $X \times B$ into Y. It follows that

$$P_y|\xi = P_{u+g(\xi,b)}|\xi, \qquad \xi\in X \qquad (6.31)$$

Suppose that $P_u|\xi$, $\xi\in X$ are dominated by Lebesgue measure on U. Then $P_{u+g(\xi,b)}|\xi$, $\xi\in X$ are similarly dominated. So condition (6.29) is satisfied by letting v_ξ be Lebesgue measure on Y.

6.2.3 Maximum likelihood estimation

Having represented a response model as a conditional likelihood problem, one may apply the analogy principle and obtain a maximum likelihood estimate of $[b, (P_u|\xi, \xi\in X)]$.

Empirical studies estimating response models by maximum likelihood have tended to impose strong restrictions on $(P_u|\xi, \xi\in X)$. The most common practice is to assert that a finite-dimensional parameter indexes all of these conditional measures. Let Γ be a finite-dimensional real space. Let $\psi(*, *)$ be a given function mapping $X \times \Gamma$

into the space of probability measures on U. It is assumed that for some γ in Γ,

$$P_u | \xi = \psi(\xi, \gamma), \qquad \xi \in X \qquad (6.32)$$

Chapters 7 and 8 will examine the asymptotic behavior of maximum likelihood estimates in this setting.

Condition (6.32) is often accompanied by the assertion that u is statistically independent of x; that is, ψ does not vary on X. Some recent theoretical studies drop condition (6.32) but retain the assertion that u is statistically independent of x. For example, Bickel (1982) analyzes the asymptotic behavior of 'adaptive' maximum likelihood estimates of a linear model. Cosslett (1983) studies maximum likelihood estimation of a binary response model. Heckman and Singer (1984) treat a survival model.

The need to either know or estimate $(P_u | \xi, \xi \in X)$ is a drawback to maximum likelihood estimation of response models, at least in applications where b is the parameter of interest. Unfortunately, it appears that response models do not generally have representations yielding less burdensome estimation methods. Alternative methods are available for models in which the response function has special characteristics. These models assume weak distributional information, yet imply moment problems involving only simple nuisance parameters. The remainder of this section presents three cases.

6.2.4 *Invertible models*

Some response models can be rewritten as models separable in the unobserved variables. Where this is so, the results of Section 6.1 apply.

Let y and u be one-to-one. That is, for each (ξ, c) in $X \times B$, let $y_0(\xi, *, c)$ be invertible as a mapping from U into Y. Let $y_0^{-1}(\xi, *, c)$ denote the inverse function mapping Y into U. Then an alternative representation of (6.24) is

$$y_0^{-1}[x(z), y(z), b] - u = 0 \qquad (6.33)$$

The separable response models (6.30) are obviously invertible. Also invertible are the simultaneous equations models prominent in the econometrics literature. In simultaneous equations analysis, (6.33) is referred to as the 'structural' model and (6.24) as the 'reduced form'.

6.2.5 Mean-independent linear models

Certain forms for the response function combine well with specific distributional restrictions. Linear response functions pair nicely with mean-independent unobservables.

Let Y and U be J-dimensional and K-dimensional real space. Let (6.24) have the linear-in-u form

$$y(z) - g_1[x(z), b] - g_2[x(z), b]u = 0 \qquad (6.34)$$

Here $g_1(*, *)$ maps $X \times B$ into R^J. The function $g_2(*, *)$ maps $X \times B$ into $R^{J \times K}$ and is written as a $J \times K$ matrix. Note that the response function in (6.34) is not invertible unless $J = K$ and the matrices $g_2(\xi, c)$, $(\xi, c) \in X \times B$ are non-singular.

Let it be known that u is mean independent of x. Let γ denote the mean of u. Equation (6.34) implies that for each ξ in X,

$$\int y \, dP_y | \xi = \int [g_1(\xi, b) + g_2(\xi, b)u] \, dP_u | \xi$$
$$= g_1(\xi, b) + g_2(\xi, b)\gamma \qquad (6.35)$$

Thus, the mean regression of y on x is $g_1(*, b) + g_2(*, b)\gamma$.

Various moment problems follow from (6.35). Orthogonality conditions may be obtained by rewriting (6.35) as

$$\int [y - g_1(\xi, b) - g_2(\xi, b)\gamma] dP_y | \xi = 0, \qquad \xi \in X \qquad (6.36)$$

Let $v(*)$ be any function on X. Then (6.36) implies that (b, γ) solves

$$\int v[x(z)] \big[y(z) - g_1[x(z), b] - g_2[x(z), b]\gamma \big]' dP = 0 \qquad (6.37)$$

Chapter 4 showed that for each component of y, the mean regression of y_j on x is the best predictor of y_j conditional on x under square loss. The results of Section 4.3 imply that for any function $w(*)$ mapping X into $(0, \infty)$ and for each $j = 1, \ldots, J$, (b, γ) solves the extremum problem

$$(b, \gamma) - \underset{(c, \delta) \in B \times \Gamma}{\text{argmin}} \int w[x(z)] \big[y_j(z) - g_{1j}[x(z), c] - g_{2j}[x(z), c]\delta \big]^2 dP$$
$$= 0 \qquad (6.38)$$

Here $g_{2j}(x, c)$ denotes the jth row of the matrix $g_2(x, c)$.

6.2.6 *Median-independent monotone models*

Whereas mean independence meshes well with linear response functions, median independence combines nicely with real-valued response functions that are monotone in a scalar u.

Let Y and U be the real line. Let it be known that u is median independent of x. Let γ denote the median of u. For each ξ in X, let $y_0(\xi, *, c)$ be non-decreasing as a function on U and continuous at γ. Then $y_0(*, \gamma, b)$ is the median regression of y on x. A proof follows.

Fix ξ. We first show that the median of $P_y|\xi$ cannot exceed $y_0(\xi, \gamma, b)$. We next show that if $y_0(\xi, *, b)$ is continuous at γ, the median cannot be smaller than $y_0(\xi, \gamma, b)$.

By monotonicity of $y_0(\xi, *, b)$ and (6.24),

$$u \leqslant \gamma \Rightarrow y_0(\xi, u, b) \leqslant y_0(\xi, \gamma, b) \Leftrightarrow y \leqslant y_0(\xi, \gamma, b) \qquad (6.39)$$

By definition of the median γ,

$$P_u[(-\infty, \gamma] | \xi] \geqslant 1/2 \qquad (6.40)$$

It follows from (6.39) and (6.40) that

$$P_y[(-\infty, y_0(\xi, \gamma, b)] | \xi] \geqslant 1/2 \qquad (6.41)$$

Hence, the median of $P_y|\xi$ cannot be larger than $y_0(\xi, \gamma, b)$.

The above holds whether or not $y_0(\xi, *, b)$ is continuous at γ. Now assume continuity. Let $\varepsilon > 0$. Then there exists an $\eta > 0$ such that

$$|u - \gamma| < \eta \Rightarrow |y_0(\xi, u, b) - y_0(\xi, \gamma, b)| < \varepsilon$$
$$\Leftrightarrow |y - y_0(\xi, \gamma, b)| < \varepsilon \qquad (6.42)$$

By (6.42) and the monotonicity of $y_0(\xi, *, b)$,

$$y \leqslant y_0(\xi, \gamma, b) - \varepsilon \Rightarrow u \leqslant \gamma - \eta \qquad (6.43)$$

By definition of the median γ,

$$P_u[(-\infty, \gamma - \eta] | \xi] < 1/2 \qquad (6.44)$$

It follows from (6.43) and (6.44) that

$$P_u[(-\infty, y_0(\xi, \gamma, b) - \varepsilon] | \xi] < 1/2 \qquad (6.45)$$

Hence, $y_0(\xi, \gamma, b) - \varepsilon$ cannot be the median of $P_y|\xi$.

Chapter 4 showed that the median regression of y on x is a best predictor of y conditional on x under absolute loss. The results of

Section 4.3 imply that for any weighting function $w(*)$, (b, γ) solves the moment extremum problem

$$(b, \gamma) - \underset{(c, \delta) \in B \times \Gamma}{\text{argmin}} \int w[x(z)] |y(z) - y_0[x(z), \delta, c]| \, dP = 0 \quad (6.46)$$

The median regression representation of median-independent monotone response models has various interesting applications. Two follow.

6.2.7 Censored response

Let $Y = [0, \infty)$ and $X = B = R^K$. Powell (1984) studies estimation of the censored linear model asserting that $y = 0$ if $x'b + u \leqslant 0$ and $y = x'b + u$ otherwise. That is,

$$y(z) - \max [0, x(z)'b + u] = 0 \quad (6.47)$$

for each ξ in X, the function $\max(0, \xi'b + *)$ is non-decreasing and continuous on U. Hence, the median of $P_y | \xi$ is $\max(0, \xi'b + \gamma)$.

Applying (6.46), (b, γ) solves

$$(b, \gamma) - \underset{(c, \delta) \in B \times \Gamma}{\text{argmin}} \int |y(z) - \max [0, x(z)'c + \delta]| \, dP = 0 \quad (6.48)$$

Applying the analogy principle to (6.48) yields the censored least absolute deviations estimate

$$(B_N, \Gamma_N) \equiv \underset{(c, \delta) \in B \times \Gamma}{\text{argmin}} \frac{1}{N} \sum_{i=1}^{N} |y_i - \max [0, x_i'c + \delta]| \quad (6.49)$$

6.2.8 Binary response

Let $Y = \{0, 1\}$ and $X = B = R^K$. Manski (1975, 1985) studies estimation of the binary response model asserting that $y = 0$ if $x'b + u \leqslant 0$ and $y = 1$ otherwise. That is,

$$y(z) - 1[x(z)'b + u > 0] = 0 \quad (6.50)$$

For each ξ in X, the response function $1[\xi'b + * > 0]$ is non-decreasing on U. For each ξ such that $\xi'b \neq -\gamma$, this function is continuous at γ. It is discontinuous at γ whenever $\xi'b = -\gamma$. Nevertheless, we can show that for all ξ, the median of $P_y | \xi$ is $1[\xi'b + \gamma > 0]$.

Fix ξ. Conditional on the event $[x = \xi]$, the median of the Bernoulli random variable y is zero if $P_y(0|\xi) \geqslant 1/2$ and one otherwise. By (6.50),

$$P_y(0|\xi) = P_u[(-\infty, -\xi'b]|\xi] \qquad (6.51)$$

It follows from the definition of the median γ and from (6.51) that

$$-\xi'b \geqslant \gamma \Leftrightarrow P_u[(-\infty, -\xi'b]|\xi] \geqslant 1/2 \Leftrightarrow P_y(0|\xi) \geqslant 1/2 \quad (6.52)$$

Hence, the median of $P_y|\xi$ is $1[\xi'b + \gamma > 0]$.

Applying (6.46), (b, γ) solves

$$(b, \gamma) - \operatorname*{argmin}_{(c,\delta) \in B \times \Gamma} \int |y(z) - 1[x(z)'c + \delta > 0]| \, dP = 0 \qquad (6.53)$$

Applying the analogy principle to (6.53) yields the maximum score estimate

$$(B_N, \Gamma_N) \equiv \operatorname*{argmin}_{(c,\delta) \in B \times \Gamma} \frac{1}{N} \sum_{i=1}^{N} |y_i - 1[x_i'c + \delta > 0]| \qquad (6.54)$$

6.2.9 Restrictions on $P_x|u$

To conclude this discussion, we call attention to an asymmetry in the traditional treatment of observed and unobserved explanatory variables in response models.

The variables x and u play identical roles in the economic process represented by the equation $y - y_0(x, u, b) = 0$. The fact that the researcher happens to observe x in no way diminishes the status of u. Structural parity suggests that distributional restrictions should be symmetric in x and u. Statistical independence possesses such symmetry. Mean and median independence do not. These conditions operate on the conditional measures $P_u|x$ but not on $P_x|u$.

One may question the practice of asserting conditional distribution restrictions in one direction only. Consider mean independence. If it is sometimes plausible to assert that u is mean independent of x, then it may also sometimes be plausible to assert that x is mean independent of u. The former and latter assertions are distinct; in a given application, one may be prepared to assert either or both. Statistical independence implies both kinds of mean independence. On the other hand, the two mean-independence conditions do not together imply statistical independence.

Asymptotic theory for method of moments estimation

Part III develops asymptotic theory for method of moments estimates. Chapter 7 presents a set of consistency theorems. Chapter 8 gives conditions implying that appropriately normalized estimates have limiting normal distributions. Chapter 9 provides further results.

In Chapter 1, we argued informally that analog estimates behave well asymptotically if two conditions are met. First, the sampling process should be such that the empirical measure P_N converges to the population measure P as $N \to \infty$. Second, the estimate should vary smoothly with P_N, at least when P_N is close to P. We must now make these notions precise.

The consistency and asymptotic normality theorems proved in Chapters 7 and 8 maintain the assumption of random sampling. These theorems concern parameter spaces that are subsets of finite-dimensional real spaces. The parts of the analysis dealing with moment equations treat finite-dimensional equations. Sections of Chapter 9 cite, but do not prove, findings on the behavior of method of moments estimates in more general settings.

At the risk of belaboring the well-appreciated, it seems worth stating explicitly why we study asymptotic theory when the typical econometric problem involves estimation from a sample of fixed size. Asymptotic theorems may or may not be relevant to analysis from a given sample. In general, these theorems have the form 'there exists (or almost surely exists) a finite sample size N_0 such that property ... holds whenever $N > N_0$.' Usually, the threshold sample size N_0 which guarantees the property of interest depends on the unknowns (b, P) and so is itself unknown. Thus, asymptotic results are relevant if the sample at hand is 'large enough', but we cannot be certain how large is large enough. This ambiguity is frustrating but seems unavoidable.

We live with the ambiguous relevance of asymptotics in part because exact sampling analysis of estimates is impractical. The impracticality is most evident when an analog estimate is obtained by implicit solution of a set of equations or an optimization problem. Then one must work very hard indeed to derive the exact sampling distribution of the estimate from knowledge of the process generating the data.

We also live with asymptotics because exact sample analysis is, in some respects, logically impossible. The sampling distribution of an analog estimate generally depends on unknown features of (b, P). Wherever this is so, one can hope only to estimate this distribution. But the sampling behavior of an estimate of the sampling distribution itself depends on unknowns. To terminate the developing sequence of estimation problems, one must resort to asymptotic arguments.

CHAPTER 7

Consistency

This chapter and the next are concerned with estimation of parameters solving finite-dimensional moment problems. The parameter
space B is a subset of K-dimensional real space. The parameter b
solves either a moment extremum problem

$$b - \underset{c \in B}{\operatorname{argmin}} \int h(z, c) \, dP = 0 \qquad (7.1)$$

or a moment equation

$$\int g(z, b) \, dP = 0 \qquad (7.2)$$

In the latter case, $g(*, *)$ takes values in J-dimensional real space. Note
that the term 'finite dimensional' does not imply that the sample space
Z is necessarily finite dimensional. In fact, most of the results we
report do not require imposition of explicit structure on Z.

In this chapter, we are concerned with the consistency of estimates
obtained by applying the analogy principle to (7.1) or (7.2). If b solves
a moment extremum problem, the method of moments estimate is

$$B_N \equiv \underset{c \in B}{\operatorname{argmin}} \int h(z, c) \, dP_N \qquad (7.3)$$

In the case of a moment equation, one selects an origin-preserving
transformation $r(*)$ mapping R^J into $[0, \infty)$. Then the estimate is

$$B_{Nr} \equiv \underset{c \in B}{\operatorname{argmin}} \, r \left[\int g(z, c) \, dP_N \right] \qquad (7.4)$$

Definitions (7.3) and (7.4) presume that the functions $\int h(z, *) \, dP_N$ and
$r[\int g(z, *) \, dP_N]$ attain their infima on B; so the estimates B_N and B_{Nr}
are non-empty. In our analysis, the existence of these estimates will be

implied by restrictions placed on the parameter space and on the functions $h(*, *)$ and $g(*, *)$.

We shall present consistency theorems for two kinds of finite-dimensional problems. These are termed 'continuous' and 'step' problems.

Continuous and step moment problems are distinguished by the behavior of $h(*, *)$ and $g(*, *)$ as functions on B. A moment extremum problem is continuous if, for each ζ in Z, $h(\zeta, *)$ is continuous on B. Similarly, a moment equation is continuous if $g(\zeta, *)$, $\zeta \in Z$ are continuous functions.

An extremum problem is step if, for each ζ in Z, $h(\zeta, *)$ is a step function taking at most two non-zero values on B. Let $v_0(*)$ and $v_1(*)$ be given functions mapping Z into the real line. Let $s(*, *)$ be a given function mapping $Z \times B$ into the real line. Then $h(*, *)$ has the form

$$h(\zeta, *) = v_0(\zeta) 1[s(\zeta, *) < 0] + v_1(\zeta) 1[s(\zeta, *) > 0], \qquad \zeta \in Z \quad (7.5)$$

A step moment equation is defined analogously, except that the functions $v_0(*)$ and $v_1(*)$ take values in R^J.

The class of continuous problems covers many applications of the moment problems examined in Part II. Empirical studies of best prediction under square loss typically assume that the best predictor of y given x is a member of a family of functions $[f(*, c), c \in B]$ mapping X into Y. Usually, the functions $f(\xi, *)$, $\xi \in X$ are continuous on B. Then the parameter b solves the continuous moment extremum problem

$$b - \underset{c \in B}{\text{argmin}} \int [y(z) - f\{x(z, c)\}]^2 \, dP = 0 \quad (7.6)$$

Analyses of the separable econometric model $u_0(z, b) - u = 0$ with mean-independent u typically make the functions $u_0(\zeta, *)$, $\zeta \in Z$ continuous on B. Then the implied orthogonality condition (see equation (6.11))

$$\int v[x(z)][u_0(z, b) - \gamma]' \, dP = 0 \quad (7.7)$$

is a continuous moment equation.

Some moment problems are inherently not continuous. One such is the orthogonality condition (equation (6.15))

$$\int v[x(z)] \, \text{sgn}[u_0(z, b) - \gamma] \, dP = 0 \quad (7.8)$$

implied by a separable econometric model with median-independent u. This is a step problem with $s[\zeta, (b, \gamma)] = u_0(\zeta, b) - \gamma$, $v_0(\zeta) = -v[x(\zeta)]$, and $v_1(\zeta) = v[x(\zeta)]$.

Another is the extremum problem (equation (6.53))

$$(b, \gamma) - \underset{(c, \delta) \in B \times \Gamma}{\mathrm{argmin}} \int |y(z) - 1[x(z)'c + \delta > 0]| \, dP = 0 \qquad (7.9)$$

implied by a binary response model with median-independent u. This step problem has $s[\zeta, (c, \delta)] = x(\zeta)'c + \delta, v_0(\zeta) = |y(\zeta)|$, and $v_1(\zeta) = |y(\zeta) - 1|$.

7.1 Preliminary theorems

This section presents a set of abstract conditions implying the almost sure (a.s.) convergence of estimates of parameters solving moment equations. We then prove a similar result for moment extremum problems. These preliminary theorems are 'bare bones' consistency findings. They give conditions that imply consistency but do not state how these conditions may be verified in applications. That task will be addressed for continuous and step problems in Sections 7.2 and 7.3 respectively.

In what follows, the symbol $| \quad |$ is used generically to denote a norm on a finite-dimensional real space. One may let $| \quad |$ be the familiar Euclidean norm but this is not necessary to the analysis. For $\delta > 0$, $B(\delta)$ is the subset of B defined by $B(\delta) \equiv [c \in B : |c - b| \geq \delta]$.

7.1.1 *Moment equations*

Let b solve a finite-dimensional moment equation. Conditions 1, 2, and 3 imply the strong consistency of a method of moments estimate. Theorem 1 states this result.

Condition 1 (Identification)
(a) There exists a unique $b \in B$ s.t. $\int g(z, b) \, dP = 0$.
(b) For each $\delta > 0$, $\underset{c \in B(\delta)}{\inf} |\int g(z, c) \, dP| > 0$.

Condition 2 (Uniform law of large numbers)

$$\lim_{N \to \infty} \sup_{c \in B} \left| \int g(z, c) \, dP_N - \int g(z, c) \, dP \right| = 0, \qquad \text{a.s}$$

Condition 3 (Origin-preserving transformation)
(a) $r(*)$ is continuous on R^J and $r(0) = 0$.
(b) For each $\varepsilon > 0$, $\inf_{|T| > \varepsilon} r(T) > 0$.

Theorem 1 Assume that Conditions 1, 2, and 3 hold and that the method of moments estimate B_{Nr} is non-empty for all N. Then

$$\lim_{N \to \infty} \sup_{c \in B_{Nr}} |c - b| = 0, \qquad \text{a.s.} \quad \blacksquare$$

PROOF   Fix $\delta > 0$. Let $\varepsilon \equiv \inf_{c \in B(\delta)} |\int g(z, c) \, dP|$. By Condition 1b, $\varepsilon > 0$. By Condition 2, there almost surely exists a finite N_1 such that

$$N > N_1 \Rightarrow \inf_{c \in B(\delta)} \left| \int g(z, c) \, dP_N \right| > \varepsilon/2$$

Let $\eta \equiv \inf_{|T| > \varepsilon/2} r(T)$. By Condition 3b, $\eta > 0$. Hence,

$$N > N_1 \Rightarrow \inf_{c \in B(\delta)} r\left[\int g(z, c) \, dP_N \right] > \eta > 0$$

Now consider $r[\int g(z, b) \, dP_N]$. By Conditions 1a, 2 and 3a, there almost surely exists a finite N_2 such that

$$N > N_2 \Rightarrow r\left[\int g(z, b) \, dP_N \right] < \eta$$

Therefore,

$$N > \max(N_1, N_2) \Rightarrow B_{Nr} \subset B - B(\delta)$$

Letting $\delta \to 0$ completes the proof.   QED.

7.1.2 Moment extremum problems

Now let b solve a finite-dimensional moment extremum problem. Replacing Conditions 1 and 2 with parallel conditions applied to $h(*, *)$ yields a parallel strong consistency theorem.

Condition 1' (Identification)
(a) ∃ a unique $b \in B$ s.t.

$$\int h(z, b) \, dP = \min_{c \in B} \int h(z, c) \, dP$$

(b) For each $\delta > 0$,

$$\inf_{c \in B(\delta)} \int h(z, c) \, dP > \int h(z, b) \, dP$$

Condition 2′ (Uniform law of large numbers)

$$\lim_{N \to \infty} \sup_{c \in B} \left| \int h(z, c) \, dP_N - \int h(z, c) \, dP \right| = 0, \qquad \text{a.s.}$$

Theorem 1′ Assume that Conditions 1′ and 2′ hold and that the method of moments estimate B_N is non-empty for all N. Then

$$\lim_{N \to \infty} \sup_{c \in B_N} |c - b| = 0, \qquad \text{a.s.} \quad \blacksquare$$

PROOF Fix $\delta > 0$. Let $H \equiv \int h(z, b) \, dP$. Let $\varepsilon \equiv \inf_{c \in B(\delta)} \int h(z, c) \, dP - H$. By Condition 1b′, $\varepsilon > 0$. By Condition 2′, there almost surely exists a finite N_1 such that

$$N > N_1 \Rightarrow \inf_{c \in B(\delta)} \int h(z, c) \, dP_N > H + \varepsilon/2$$

Now consider $\int h(z, b) \, dP_N$. By Conditions 1a′ and 2′, there almost surely exists a finite N_2 such that

$$N > N_2 \Rightarrow \int h(z, b) \, dP_N < H + \varepsilon/2$$

Therefore,

$$N > \max (N_1, N_2) \Rightarrow B_N \subset B - B(\delta)$$

Letting $\delta \to 0$ completes the proof.   Q.E.D.

7.1.3 *The identification assumption*

Theorems 1 and 1′ lay bare the essential requirements for an estimator to be consistent. Let us consider the role played by each of the conditions of Theorem 1. (Theorem 1′ can be interpreted in similar fashion.)

Condition 1a states that the parameter b is identified. Clearly, consistent estimation of b requires that the asserted moment equation

have a unique solution. If no solution exists, the estimation problem
has been misspecified and b is not defined. If the equation has multiple
solutions, sample data cannot possibly distinguish between them.

There is no general approach to verification of Condition 1a. To
understand why, simply observe that the restriction $\int g(z, b) \, dP = 0$ is a
system of nonlinear equations. Applied mathematics provides no
general constructive methods for determining the number of solutions to such systems. One must proceed more or less case by case.

Condition 1b is a uniformity requirement that strengthens the
sense in which b is distinguished from all other points in B.
Condition 1a implies that $|\int g(z, c) \, dP| > 0$ for all $c \neq b$ but does not
foreclose the possibility that for some $\delta > 0$,

$$\inf_{c \in B(\delta)} \left| \int g(z, c) \, dP \right| = 0 \tag{7.10}$$

That is, there may exist parameter values whose distances from b are
greater than δ, yet which almost solve the moment equation.

This would not be a concern if we knew the true population
moment function $\int g(z, *) \, dP$. In that ideal situation, any deviation of
$\int g(z, c) \, dP$ from zero, no matter how small, suffices to distinguish c
from b. In practice, however, we attempt to learn b from analysis of the
sample moment function $\int g(z, *) \, dP_N$. This function almost always
differs from $\int g(z, *) \, dP$. If (7.10) holds, we cannot rely on $\int g(z, *) \, dP_N$ to
appropriately distinguish b from every point in the disjoint set $B(\delta)$,
even if $\int g(z, *) \, dP_N$ is very close to $\int g(z, *) \, dP$. So Condition 1b, which
disallows (7.10), seems necessary for consistent estimation. We shall
later prove lemmas showing that Condition 1b is satisfied in both
continuous and step moment equations, provided that certain
regularity conditions hold.

7.1.4 Laws of large numbers

Condition 2 formalizes the requirement that P_N be an appropriate
sample analog for P. The condition requires that a uniform strong law
of large numbers hold. A 'law of large numbers' is a theorem showing
that $\int g(z, *) \, dP_N$ converges to $\int g(z, *) \, dP$, in some sense. Strong laws
show that the convergence holds in almost every infinite sample
sequence $z_i, i = 1, \ldots, \infty$ and thus yield strong consistency theorems.
An alternative form of Condition 2 would require only that
$\int g(z, *) \, dP_N$ approach $\int g(z, *) \, dP$ weakly, that is in probability. In that

case, we would obtain a weak consistency version of Theorem 1.

The classical versions of the strong law of large numbers (see, for example, Rao, 1973, Chapter 2) imply only pointwise convergence of $\int g(z, *) \, dP_N$ to $\int g(z, *) \, dP$. That is, they show that for each c in B, $\int g(z, c) \, dP_N$ converges almost surely to $\int g(z, c) \, dP$. Condition 2 imposes the stricter requirement that the convergence be uniform on B.

It is important to understand why pointwise convergence of $\int g(z, *) \, dP_N$ to $\int g(z, *) \, dP$ is not enough for consistent estimation. Pointwise convergence means that for every $\eta > 0$ and c in B, there almost surely exists a finite sample size $N_{\eta c}$ such that

$$\left| \int g(z, c) \, dP_N - \int g(z, c) \, dP \right| < \eta$$

for all $N > N_{\eta c}$. Combined with Condition 1a, pointwise convergence implies that for each $c \neq b$, $\int g(z, c) \, dP_N$ is almost surely further from zero than is $\int g(z, b) \, dP_N$, provided that N is large enough. But the sample size required to guarantee this may vary with c. Thus, it remains possible that for some $\delta > 0$ and for all finite N,

$$\inf_{c \in B(\delta)} \left| \int g(z, c) \, dP_N \right| = 0 \qquad (7.11)$$

In this event, sample data cannot distinguish b from the disjoint set $B(\delta)$, no matter how large N is.

Condition 2 disallows (7.11) by requiring that the convergence be uniform on B. That is, it asserts the almost sure existence of a finite sample size N_η such that $|\int g(z, c) \, dP_N - \int g(z, c) \, dP| < \eta$ for all $N > N_\eta$ and all c in B. Combined with Condition 1b, uniform convergence implies that for each $\delta > 0$, all the moment values $\int g(z, c) \, dP_N$, $c \in B(\delta)$ are simultaneously further from zero than is $\int g(z, b) \, dP_N$, provided that N is large enough. We shall later give lemmas showing that under random sampling, both continuous and step moment problems satisfy Condition 2, if certain regularity conditions hold.

7.1.5 Transformations

Condition 3 indicates that any reasonable transformation $r(*)$ is compatible with consistent estimation. Given Conditions 1 and 2, Condition 3a implies that

$$\lim_{N \to \infty} r\left[\int g(z, b) \, dP_N \right] = r\left[\int g(z, b) \, dP \right] = 0, \qquad \text{a.s.} \quad (7.12)$$

Condition 3b has the same purpose as Condition 1b. Note that one has freedom to select $r(*)$, so one can always ensure that Condition 3 is satisfied.

7.1.6 *Finite parameter spaces*

It is of interest to observe that when the parameter space contains finitely many points, the conditions for consistency simplify substantially. In this case, Condition 1a implies 1b. Pointwise convergence in Condition 2 implies uniform convergence. Condition 3b reduces to the statement $r(T) > 0$ for $T \neq 0$. Thus, all of the uniformity requirements in Conditions 1–3 are safeguards against irregularities that can occur only when B is infinite. Of course B generally is infinite in applications so these safeguards are necessary.

7.2   Continuous problems

Let us now apply Theorems 1 and 1' to continuous moment problems. It suffices to consider in detail the case of moment equations. This done, parallel findings for extremum problems follow immediately.

7.2.1 *Moment equations*

To apply Theorem 1, we need to show that the estimate B_{N}, exists and to verify Conditions 1, 2, and 3. We have noted that Condition 1a can only be checked case by case and that one can ensure Condition 3 by suitable choice of $r(*)$. So the analysis will focus on the existence of estimates and on verification of Conditions 1b and 2.

Four assumptions will be maintained. These are:

Condition 4 (Continuity)
For each $\zeta \in Z$, $g(\zeta, *)$ is continuous on B.

Condition 5 (Boundedness)
There exists a function $D(*)$ mapping Z into $[0, \infty)$ such that
 (i) The integral $\int D(z)\, dP$ exists and is finite.
(ii) $|g(\zeta, c)| \leqslant D(\zeta)$ for all (ζ, c) in $Z \times B$.

Condition 6 (Compactness)
The parameter space B is compact.

Condition 7 (Random sampling)
The observations z_i, $i = 1, \ldots, \infty$ are independent realizations from P.

Lemmas 1 through 3 and Theorems 2 and 2′ give the results. Discussion of Conditions 4 through 7 then follows.

Lemma 1
Conditions 3a, 4, and 6 imply that the estimate B_{Nr} exists. ■

PROOF By Condition 4, $\int g(z, *) dP_N \equiv (1/N) \sum_{i=1}^N g(z_i, *)$ is the sum of finitely many continuous functions and so is itself continuous on B. By Condition 3a, $r[\int g(z, *) dP_N]$ is continuous on B. By Condition 6, B is compact. A real-valued continuous function on a compact set attains its infimum. So B_{Nr} is non-empty. Q.E.D.

Lemma 2
Conditions 4 and 5 imply that $\int g(z, *) dP$ is continuous on B. Given continuity of $\int g(z, *) dP$, Conditions 1a and 6 imply Condition 1b. ■

PROOF Continuity of $\int g(z, *) dP$ is a consequence of the Lebesgue bounded convergence theorem:

Let v be a measure on Z. Let $f_j(*)$, $j = 1, \ldots, \infty$ be a sequence of functions on Z converging pointwise to a limit $f(*)$. Suppose that there exists a function $D(*)$ on Z such that
  (i) the integral $\int D(z) dv$ exists and is finite;
  (ii) $|f_j(\zeta)| \leq D(\zeta)$ for every integer j and each ζ in Z.
Then the integrals $\int f(z) dv$ and $\int f_j(z) dv$, $j = 1, \ldots, \infty$ exist and $\lim_{j \to \infty} \int f_j(z) dv = \int f(z) dv$.

See Kolmogorov and Fomin (1970, p. 303) for a proof.

To apply this fundamental result, let c be any point in B and let $c_j, j = 1, \ldots, \infty$ be any sequence of points in B converging to c. The continuity assumed in Condition 4 implies that

$$j \to \infty \Rightarrow g(\zeta, c_j) \to g(\zeta, c), \qquad \zeta \in Z$$

So the sequence $g(*, c_j)$, $j = 1, \ldots, \infty$ converges pointwise to the limit $g(*, c)$. The boundedness assumed in Condition 5 implies the existence of a function $D(*)$ such that $\int D(z) dP$ exists and $|g(\zeta, c_j)| \leq D(\zeta)$ for each

j and ζ. Hence the bounded convergence theorem implies that

$$\lim_{j \to \infty} \int g(z, c_j) \, dP = \int g(z, c) \, dP$$

This holds for all points c in B and for all sequences $\{c_j\}$ converging to c. It follows that $\int g(z, *) \, dP$ is continuous on B.

We may now prove that Condition 1b holds. Norms are continuous functions; so continuity of $\int g(z, *) \, dP$ implies continuity of $|\int g(z, *) \, dP|$. The set $B(\delta)$ is a closed subset of the compact set B; so $B(\delta)$ is compact. Hence, $|\int g(z, *) \, dP|$ attains its infimum on $B(\delta)$. Let c_0 minimize $|\int g(z, *) \, dP|$ on $B(\delta)$. By Condition 1a, $|\int g(z, c_0) \, dP| > 0$. It follows that

$$\min_{c \in B(\delta)} \left| \int g(z, c) \, dP \right| > 0. \qquad\qquad \text{Q.E.D.}$$

Lemma 3
Conditions 4, 5, 6, and 7 imply Condition 2. ∎

PROOF We first need to state some preliminary facts and introduce notation.

The proof uses the fact that a continuous function on a compact set is uniformly continuous. So the functions $g(\zeta, *), \zeta \in Z$ are all uniformly continuous on B. This implies that for each ζ in Z and every $\eta > 0$, there exists a $\delta_{\zeta\eta} > 0$ such that

$$|a - c| < \delta_{\zeta\eta} \Rightarrow |g(\zeta, a) - g(\zeta, c)| < \eta, \qquad (a, c) \in B \times B \quad (7.13)$$

Fix η. For $\lambda > 0$, define the set $Z(\eta, \lambda) \equiv [\zeta \in Z : \lambda < \delta_{\zeta\eta}]$. It follows from (7.13) that for each ζ in $Z(\eta, \lambda)$,

$$|a - c| < \lambda \Rightarrow |g(\zeta, a) - g(\zeta, c)| < \eta, \qquad (a, c) \in B \times B \quad (7.14)$$

The proof uses the fact that as λ shrinks to zero, $Z(\eta, \lambda)$ expands to the full sample space Z. This implies the existence of a $\lambda_\eta > 0$ such that

$$\lambda \leqslant \lambda_\eta \Rightarrow \int_{Z - Z(\eta, \lambda_\eta)} D(z) \, dP < \eta \quad (7.15)$$

where $D(*)$ is the bounding function of Condition 5 and where $Z - Z(\eta, \lambda_\eta)$ is the complement of the set $Z(\eta, \lambda_\eta)$. (Actually, $Z(\eta, \lambda_\eta)$ may not be measurable. If so, (7.15) is to be interpreted as stating that the upper integral of $D(*)$ on $Z - Z(\eta, \lambda_\eta)$ is less than η. We shall ignore measurability considerations henceforth.)

With the above as background, observe that for all pairs (a, c) in $B \times B$, application of the triangle inequality yields

$$\left| \int g(z, a) \, dP_N - \int g(z, a) \, dP \right| = \left| \int [g(z, a) - g(z, c)] \, dP_N \right.$$

$$\left. - \int [g(z, a) - g(z, c)] \, dP + \left[\int g(z, c) \, dP_N - \int g(z, c) \, dP \right] \right|$$

$$\leqslant \int |g(z, a) - g(z, c)| \, dP_N + \int |g(z, a) - g(z, c)| \, dP$$

$$+ \left| \int g(z, c) \, dP_N - \int g(z, c) \, dP \right| \tag{7.16}$$

Now fix $c \in B$ and $\eta > 0$. Let $\lambda = \lambda_\eta$. It follows from (7.14), (7.15), the triangle inequality, and Condition 5 that for $a \in B$ such that $|a - c| < \lambda_\eta$,

$$\int |g(z, a) - g(z, c)| \, dP$$

$$= \int_{Z(\eta, \lambda_\eta)} |g(z, a) - g(z, c)| \, dP + \int_{Z - Z(\eta, \lambda_\eta)} |g(z, a) - g(z, c)| \, dP$$

$$\leqslant \int_{Z(\eta, \lambda_\eta)} \eta \, dP + 2 \int_{Z - Z(\eta, \lambda_\eta)} D(z) \, dP \leqslant 3\eta \tag{7.17}$$

By the same reasoning,

$$\int |g(z, a) - g(z, c)| \, dP_N$$

$$= \int_{Z(\eta, \lambda_\eta)} |g(z, a) - g(z, c)| \, dP_N + \int_{Z - Z(\eta, \lambda_\eta)} |g(z, a) - g(z, c)| \, dP_N$$

$$\leqslant \int_{Z(\eta, \lambda_\eta)} \eta \, dP_N + 2 \int_{Z - Z(\eta, \lambda_\eta)} D(z) \, dP_N$$

$$\leqslant \eta + 2 \int_{Z - Z(\eta, \lambda_\eta)} D(z) \, dP_N \tag{7.18}$$

The assumption of random sampling in Condition 7 implies, by the strong law of large numbers, the almost sure existence of a finite sample size $N_{1\eta}$ such that

$$N > N_{1\eta} \Rightarrow \left| \int_{z-Z(\eta,\lambda_\eta)} D(z)\,dP_N - \int_{z-Z(\eta,\lambda_\eta)} D(z)\,dP \right| < \eta \quad (7.19)$$

Hence, by (7.15), (7.18), and (7.19),

$$N > N_{1\eta} \Rightarrow \int |g(z,a) - g(z,c)|\,dP_N \leqslant 5\eta \quad (7.20)$$

It now follows from (7.16) through (7.20) that for $N > N_{1\eta}$ and for $a \in B$ such that $|a - c| < \lambda_\eta$,

$$\left| \int g(z,a)\,dP_N - \int g(z,a)\,dP \right| \leqslant 8\eta + \left| \int g(z,c)\,dP_N - \int g(z,c)\,dP \right| \quad (7.21)$$

The space B, being compact, has a finite λ_η-cover. That is, B has a finite subset B_η such that, given any $a \in B$, at least one element of B_η is within distance λ_η of a. It follows from this and from (7.21) that for $N > N_{1\eta}$ and for all $a \in B$,

$$\left| \int g(z,a)\,dP_N - \int g(z,a)\,dP \right| \leqslant 8\eta + \max_{c \in B_\eta} \left| \int g(z,c)\,dP_N - \int g(z,c)\,dP \right| \quad (7.22)$$

Condition 7 and the strong law of large numbers imply that there almost surely exists a finite $N_{2\eta}$ such that

$$N > N_{2\eta} \Rightarrow \max_{c \in B_\eta} \left| \int g(z,c)\,dP_N - \int g(z,c)\,dP \right| < \eta \quad (7.23)$$

Equations (7.22) and (7.23) imply that for $N > \max(N_{1\eta}, N_{2\eta})$ and all $a \in B$,

$$\left| \int g(z,a)\,dP_N - \int g(z,a)\,dP \right| \leqslant 9\eta \quad (7.24)$$

The bound (7.24) holds for all $a \in B$; hence,

$$\sup_{a \in B} \left| \int g(z,a)\,dP_N - \int g(z,a)\,dP \right| \leqslant 9\eta \quad (7.25)$$

Letting $\eta \to 0$ proves the lemma.   Q.E.D.

Theorem 2
Assume that Conditions 1a, 3, 4, 5, 6, and 7 hold. Then B_{Nr} is

non-empty for all N and

$$\lim_{\substack{N \to \infty \\ c \in B_{Nr}}} \sup |c - b| = 0, \qquad \text{a.s.} \quad \blacksquare$$

PROOF This strong consistency theorem follows immediately from Theorem 1 and from Lemmas 1 through 3.   Q.E.D.

7.2.2 Moment extremum problems

A parallel consistency theorem may be proved for moment extremum problems. Replacing Conditions 4 and 5 by similar conditions applied to $h(*, *)$ yields results that parallel Lemmas 1, 2, and 3. We omit the details.

Condition 4' (Continuity)
For each $\zeta \in Z$, $h(\zeta, *)$ is continuous on B.

Condition 5' (Boundedness)
There exists a function $D(*)$ mapping Z into $[0, \infty)$ such that
(i) the integral $\int D(z) dP$ exists and is finite.
(ii) $|h(\zeta, c)| \leqslant D(\zeta)$ for all (ζ, c) in $Z \times B$.

Theorem 2'
Assume that Conditions 1a', 4', 5', 6, and 7 hold. Then B_N is non-empty for all N and

$$\lim_{\substack{N \to \infty \\ c \in B_N}} \sup |c - b| = 0, \quad \text{a.s.} \quad \blacksquare$$

7.2.3 The continuity and boundedness assumptions

Conditions 4 and 5 provide regularity that makes the population moment function $\int g(z, *) dP$ continuous on B and makes the sample moment function $\int g(z, *) dP_N$ behave like $\int g(z, *) dP$ as N grows. It is important to recognize that Condition 4 alone does not suffice. Continuity of the functions $g(\zeta, *)$, $\zeta \in Z$ does not by itself imply continuity of $\int g(z, *) dP$. Nor does it imply a uniform law of large numbers.

Although the combination of Conditions 4 and 5 is sufficient to ensure well-behaved asymptotics, neither condition is essential. The step moment problems to be examined in Section 7.3 are not continuous. The analysis of linear models in Chapter 8 covers a case in which boundedness is violated.

Note that Conditions 4 and 6 imply part (ii) of Condition 5; a continuous function on a compact set is always bounded. The non-redundant part of Condition 5 is the assumption (i) that the bounding function $D(*)$ is integrable.

7.2.4 *The compactness assumption*

Lemmas 1, 2, and 3 all make use of the assumption that B is compact. Consistency theorems specifying a compact parameter space are useful provided that one has information bounding the location of b within R^K. Consistency theorems not requiring compactness of B can be proved for moment problems imposing special structure on the functions $g(*, *)$ and $h(*, *)$. For example, we shall show in Chapter 8 that Conditions 5 and 6 are both unnecessary if $g(*, *)$ is a linear function on B. Considering problems in which B is the real line, Huber (1981, Chapter 6) provides consistency theorems for moment equations in which $g(\zeta, *)$, $\zeta \in Z$ are monotone functions on B.

7.2.5 *The random sampling assumption*

Theorems 2 and 2' rely on the assumption of random sampling through Lemma 3. Jennrich (1969) stated a more general version of this uniform law of large numbers. His Theorem 1 assumes that the observations z_i, $i = 1, \ldots, \infty$ are independent drawings from a sequence of probability measures P_i, $i = 1, \ldots, \infty$. Random sampling is the special case in which these measures coincide.

Uniform laws of large numbers have become basic tools of econometric analysis. The literature now offers many versions. Pollard (1984) covers the random sampling setting in great generality. Amemiya (1985), Andrews (1987), and Gallant (1987) provide results for independent sampling from a sequence of probability measures and for various dependent sampling processes.

7.3 Step problems

This section applies Theorems 1 and 1' to step moment problems. The development parallels that of Section 7.2. Considering step equations, we present conditions implying lemmas analogous to Lemmas 1 through 3. These lemmas then imply a consistency theorem analogous to Theorem 2. The same arguments show consistency for estimates in extremum problems.

Asymptotic analysis of step problem estimation is more subtle than the corresponding analysis for continuous problems. The analysis of Section 7.2 made critical use of the finding in Lemma 2 that the population moment function $\int g(z, *)\, dP$ is continuous on B. But a step function specification for $g(\zeta, *)$, $\zeta \in Z$ would seem to imply that $\int g(z, *)\, dP$ is itself a step function.

In fact, step problems may have continuous population moment functions. To grasp the idea, let $c \in B$ and let Z_c denote the set of points ζ in Z for which $g(\zeta, *)$ is discontinuous at c. If the set Z_c has probability zero under P, it is plausible that $\int g(z, *)\, dP$ is continuous at c. It turns out that the condition $P(Z_c) = 0$ does not quite imply that $\int g(z, *)\, dP$ is continuous at c; continuity requires that this assumption be combined with others. Lemma 5 will show that if P and $g(*, *)$ are suitably regular, then $\int g(z, *)\, dP$ is continuous on B.

7.3.1 Moment equations

Our treatment of step equations maintains many of the conditions imposed on continuous equations. As in Section 7.2, we assume that b is identified (Condition 1a), that $r(*)$ is well-behaved (Condition 3), that B is compact (Condition 6), and that the data are a random sample (Condition 7).

We replace the continuity and boundedness assumptions of Conditions 4 and 5 with the following two assumptions.

Condition 8 (*Step equicontinuity*)
(a) $g(\zeta, *) = v_0(\zeta) 1[s(\zeta, *) < 0] + v_1(\zeta) 1[s(\zeta, *) > 0]$, $\zeta \in Z$ where $s(*, *)$ maps $Z \times B$ into R^1 and $v_0(*)$ and $v_1(*)$ map Z into R^J.
(b) The functions $s(\zeta, *)$, $\zeta \in Z$ are equicontinuous on B.

Condition 9 (*Boundary*)

$$\limsup_{\alpha \to 0} \int_{Z_{c\alpha}} |v_0(z)|\, dP = \limsup_{\alpha \to 0} \int_{Z_{c\alpha}} |v_1(z)|\, dP = 0$$

where $Z_{c\alpha} \equiv [\zeta \in Z: -\alpha < s(\zeta, c) < \alpha]$.

These conditions warrant some explanation before we proceed to use them. Part (a) of Condition 8 defines a step equation. Part (b) requires that the functions $s(\zeta, *)$, $\zeta \in Z$ be appropriately smooth. These functions are said to be equicontinuous on B if, for every $\alpha > 0$, there exists a $\delta_\alpha > 0$ such that

$$|a - c| < \delta_\alpha \Rightarrow |s(\zeta, a) - s(\zeta, c)| < \alpha, \qquad (\zeta, a, c) \in Z \times B \times B$$

Thus, equicontinuity on B is continuity on B that is uniform with respect to both arguments of $s(*, *)$. In contrast, continuity without such uniformity requires only that, for each (ζ, c) in $Z \times B$ and $\alpha > 0$, there exist a $\delta_{\zeta c \alpha} > 0$ such that

$$|a - c| < \delta_{\zeta c \alpha} \Rightarrow |s(\zeta, a) - s(\zeta, c)| < \alpha, \qquad a \in B$$

Condition 9 formalizes the earlier heuristic remark that, for each c in B, the set Z_c of points for which $g(\zeta, *)$ is discontinuous at c should have probability zero under P. The condition essentially requires that there be probability zero of drawing a ζ such that $s(\zeta, c) = 0$ and only small probability of drawing a ζ such that $s(\zeta, c)$ is close to zero. The reason for the precise form of Condition 9 will become apparent in the proofs of Lemmas 5 and 6.

Lemmas 4 through 6 and Theorems 3 and 3′ give the results. Further discussion of Conditions 8 and 9 then follows.

Lemma 4
Condition 8a implies that the estimate B_{Nr} exists. ■

PROOF   For each $i = 1, \ldots, N$, the function $g(z_i, *)$ can take only three values on B, namely $v_0(z_i)$, 0, and $v_1(z_i)$. Hence $\int g(z, *) dP_N$ can take only finitely many values on B. It follows that $r[\int g(z, *) dP_N]$ attains its infimum on B.   Q.E.D.

Lemma 5
Conditions 8 and 9 imply that $\int g(z, *) dP$ is continuous on B. Given continuity of $\int g(z, *) dP$, Conditions 1a and 6 imply Condition 1b. ■

PROOF   It suffices to prove the first statement. The second statement has already been proved in Lemma 2.

To show continuity of $\int g(z, *) dP$, observe that for each $(a, c) \in B \times B$,

$$\left| \int g(z, a) dP - \int g(z, c) dP \right|$$

$$= \left| \int v_0(z) \left[1[s(z, a) < 0] - 1[s(z, c) < 0] \right] dP \right|$$

$$+ \int v_1(z) \left[1[s(z,a) > 0] - 1[s(z,c) > 0] \right] dP \bigg|$$

$$\leqslant \int |v_0(z) \left[1[s(z,a) < 0] - 1[s(z,c) < 0] \right]| \, dP$$

$$+ \int |v_1(z) \left[1[s(z,a) > 0] - 1[s(z,c) > 0] \right]| \, dP$$

$$\leqslant \int_{Z(a,c)} |v_0(z)| \, dP + \int_{Z(a,c)} |v_1(z)| \, dP \qquad (7.26)$$

where $Z(a,c) \equiv [\zeta \in Z: s(\zeta,a) \leqslant 0 \leqslant s(\zeta,c) \cup s(\zeta,a) \geqslant 0 \geqslant s(\zeta,c)]$.

Fix $c \in B$ and let $\alpha > 0$. Condition 8b implies the existence of a $\delta_\alpha > 0$ such that

$$|a - c| < \delta_\alpha \Rightarrow |s(\zeta,a) - s(\zeta,c)| < \alpha, \qquad \zeta \in Z \qquad (7.27)$$

Hence, for all $a \in B$ such that $|a - c| < \delta_\alpha$ and for all $\zeta \in Z$,

$$s(\zeta,c) > \alpha \Rightarrow s(\zeta,a) > 0 \qquad \text{and} \qquad s(\zeta,c) < -\alpha \Rightarrow s(\zeta,a) < 0$$

$$(7.28)$$

By (7.28) and the definition of $Z(a,c)$,

$$|a - c| < \delta_\alpha \Rightarrow Z(a,c) \subset Z_{c\alpha} \qquad (7.29)$$

where $Z_{c\alpha} \equiv [\zeta \in Z: -\alpha < s(\zeta,c) < \alpha]$ as in Condition 9. Therefore, by (7.26),

$$|a - c| < \delta_\alpha \Rightarrow \left| \int g(z,a) \, dP - \int g(z,c) \, dP \right|$$

$$\leqslant \int_{Z_{c\alpha}} |v_0(z)| \, dP + \int_{Z_{c\alpha}} |v_1(z)| \, dP \qquad (7.30)$$

Now select an $\varepsilon > 0$. By Condition 9, there is an $\alpha(\varepsilon) > 0$ such that

$$\alpha \leqslant \alpha(\varepsilon) \Rightarrow \int_{Z_{c\alpha}} |v_0(z)| \, dP + \int_{Z_{c\alpha}} |v_1(z)| \, dP < \varepsilon \qquad (7.31)$$

It follows from (7.30) and (7.31) that

$$|a - c| < \delta_{\alpha(\varepsilon)} \Rightarrow \left| \int g(z,a) \, dP - \int g(z,c) \, dP \right| < \varepsilon \qquad (7.32)$$

This proves that $\int g(z, *) \mathrm{d}P$ is continuous at c. Recall that c was any point in B; hence $\int g(z, *) \mathrm{d}P$ is continuous on B.   Q.E.D.

Note that Lemma 5 does not require the uniformity part of Condition 9. It is enough that for each c in B,

$$\lim_{\alpha \to 0} \int_{Z_{c\alpha}} |v_0(z)| \, \mathrm{d}P = \lim_{\alpha \to 0} \int_{Z_{c\alpha}} |v_1(z)| \, \mathrm{d}P = 0$$

The uniformity condition will be used in the proof of Lemma 6.

Lemma 6
Conditions 6, 7, 8, and 9 imply Condition 2.   ∎

PROOF As in the proof of Lemma 3, the triangle inequality implies that for all pairs (a, c) in $B \times B$,

$$\left| \int g(z, a) \mathrm{d}P_N - \int g(z, a) \mathrm{d}P \right|$$

$$= \left| \int [g(z, a) - g(z, c)] \mathrm{d}P_N - \int [g(z, a) - g(z, c)] \mathrm{d}P \right.$$

$$\left. + \left[\int g(z, c) \mathrm{d}P_N - \int g(z, c) \mathrm{d}P \right] \right|$$

$$\leqslant \int |g(z, a) - g(z, c)| \mathrm{d}P_N + \int |g(z, a) - g(z, c)| \mathrm{d}P$$

$$+ \left| \int g(z, c) \mathrm{d}P_N - \int g(z, c) \mathrm{d}P \right| \qquad (7.33)$$

Fix $c \in B$ and let $\alpha > 0$. The proof of Lemma 5 showed the existence of a $\delta_\alpha > 0$ such that (see (7.30))

$$|a - c| < \delta_\alpha \Rightarrow \left| \int g(z, a) \mathrm{d}P - \int g(z, c) \mathrm{d}P \right|$$

$$\leqslant \int_{Z_{c\alpha}} |v_0(z)| \, \mathrm{d}P + \int_{Z_{c\alpha}} |v_1(z)| \, \mathrm{d}P \qquad (7.34)$$

The same inequality holds if P_N replaces P. Therefore, by (7.33) and (7.34),

$$|a - c| < \delta_\alpha \Rightarrow \left| \int g(z, a) \mathrm{d}P_N - \int g(z, a) \mathrm{d}P \right|$$

$$\leqslant \int_{Z_{c\alpha}} |v_0(z)| \mathrm{d}P_N + \int_{Z_{c\alpha}} |v_1(z)| \mathrm{d}P_N$$

$$+ \int_{Z_{c\alpha}} |v_0(z)| \mathrm{d}P + \int_{Z_{c\alpha}} |v_1(z)| \mathrm{d}P$$

$$+ \left| \int g(z, c) \mathrm{d}P_N - \int g(z, c) \mathrm{d}P \right| \tag{7.35}$$

The space B is compact. Hence B has a finite subset B_α such that, given any $a \in B$, at least one element of B_α is within distance δ_α of a. It follows from this and from (7.35) that for all $a \in B$,

$$\left| \int g(z, a) \mathrm{d}P_N - \int g(z, a) \mathrm{d}P \right|$$

$$\leqslant \max_{c \in B_\alpha} \int_{Z_{c\alpha}} |v_0(z)| \mathrm{d}P_N + \max_{c \in B_\alpha} \int_{Z_{c\alpha}} |v_1(z)| \mathrm{d}P_N$$

$$+ \max_{c \in B_\alpha} \int_{Z_{c\alpha}} |v_0(z)| \mathrm{d}P + \max_{c \in B_\alpha} \int_{Z_{c\alpha}} |v_1(z)| \mathrm{d}P$$

$$+ \max_{c \in B_\alpha} \left| \int g(z, c) \mathrm{d}P_N - \int g(z, c) \mathrm{d}P \right| \tag{7.36}$$

The bound on the right-hand side of (7.36) holds for all $a \in B$; so proof of the lemma requires only that this bound be made arbitrarily small. Let $N \to \infty$. Condition 7 and the strong law of large numbers imply that

$$\max_{c \in B_\alpha} \left| \int g(z, c) \mathrm{d}P_N - \int g(z, c) \mathrm{d}P \right| \to 0, \qquad \text{a.s.} \tag{7.37}$$

and also that

$$\max_{c \in B_\alpha} \int_{Z_{c\alpha}} |v_0(z)| \mathrm{d}P_N + \max_{c \in B_\alpha} \int_{Z_{c\alpha}} |v_1(z)| \mathrm{d}P_N$$

$$\to \max_{c \in B_\alpha} \int_{Z_{c\alpha}} |v_0(z)| \mathrm{d}P + \max_{c \in B_\alpha} \int_{Z_{c\alpha}} |v_1(z)| \mathrm{d}P, \qquad \text{a.s.} \tag{7.38}$$

It follows that for every $\alpha > 0$ and $\eta > 0$, there is a finite $N_{\alpha\eta}$ such that

$$N > N_{\alpha\eta} \Rightarrow \sup_{a \in B} \left| \int g(z,a) dP_N - \int g(z,a) dP \right|$$

$$\leqslant 2 \left[\max_{c \in B_\alpha} \int_{Z_{c\alpha}} |v_0(z)| dP + \max_{c \in B_\alpha} \int_{Z_{c\alpha}} |v_1(z)| dP \right] + \eta$$

$$\leqslant 2 \left[\sup_{c \in B} \int_{Z_{c\alpha}} |v_0(z)| dP + \sup_{c \in B} \int_{Z_{c\alpha}} |v_1(z)| dP \right] + \eta \qquad (7.39)$$

Letting $(\alpha, \eta) \to 0$ and applying Condition 9 completes the proof.

Q.E.D.

Theorem 3
Assume that Conditions 1a, 3, 6, 7, 8, and 9 hold. Then B_{Nr} is non-empty for all N and

$$\lim_{N \to \infty} \sup_{c \in B_{Nr}} |c - b| = 0, \qquad \text{a.s.} \quad \blacksquare$$

PROOF This strong consistency theorem follows immediately from Theorem 1 and from Lemmas 4 through 6.

Q.E.D.

7.3.2 *Moment extremum problems*

A parallel theorem may be proved for moment extremum problems. Simply replace Condition 8 by the following.

Condition 8′ (Step equicontinuity)
(a) $h(\zeta, *) = v_0(\zeta) 1[s(\zeta, *) < 0] + v_1(\zeta) 1[s(\zeta, *) > 0]$, $\zeta \in Z$ where $s(*, *)$ maps $Z \times B$ into R^1 and $v_0(*)$ and $v_1(*)$ map Z into R^1.
(b) The functions $s(\zeta, *)$, $\zeta \in Z$ are equicontinuous on B.

Theorem 3′
Assume that Conditions 1a′, 6, 7, 8′, and 9 hold. Then B_N is non-empty for all N and

$$\lim_{N \to \infty} \sup_{c \in B_N} |c - b| = 0, \qquad \text{a.s.} \quad \blacksquare$$

7.3.3 *The step function assumption*

Lemma 4 calls attention to the fact that in a step moment equation, the sample moment function $\int g(z, *)dP_N$ can take on only finitely many values on B. This implies that the method of moments estimate B_{Nr} is generally set-valued. The same conclusion holds for the estimate B_N in a step extremum problem.

In Chapter 1, we noted that although the literature focusses on point estimation, the analogy principle gives no reason to isolate one element of a set-valued estimate for special attention. This observation warrants reiteration. The statements of Theorems 3 and 3' make no reference to the cardinality of the estimates B_{Nr} and B_N, except that they should be non-empty. Consistency requires only that these set-valued estimates shrink almost surely towards the point b as $N \to \infty$.

7.3.4 The equicontinuity assumption

Theorems 3 and 3' are useful to the extent that step problems of applied interest satisfy the equicontinuity and boundary assumptions specified in Conditions 8b and 9.

The equicontinuity assumption need hold only for some sign-equivalent version of $s(*, *)$. Observe that the step functions $g(\zeta, *)$, $\zeta \in Z$ are unchanged if $s(*, *)$ is replaced by $\text{sgn}[s(*, *)]$. Hence Condition 8b does not really require that $s(*, *)$ be equicontinuous. It is enough that there exist an equicontinuous, sign-preserving function of $s(*, *)$.

We shall use this fact in the proof of Lemma 7. Lemma 7 states three easily checked conditions, any one of which implies Condition 8b.

Lemma 7
Let Condition 6 hold. Then Condition 8b is satisfied if

(a) $Z \times B$ is a compact metric space and $s(*, *)$ is continuous on $Z \times B$; or
(b) there exists an open convex set $C \subset R^K$ such that $B \subset C$, $s(*, *)$ is bounded on $Z \times C$, and $s(\zeta, *)$, $\zeta \in Z$ are convex functions on C; or

(c) $s(\zeta, c) = x(\zeta)'c$, $(\zeta, c) \in Z \times B$,

   where $x(*)$ maps Z into R^K.

PROOF (a) A continuous function on a compact metric space is uniformly continuous. Uniform continuity on $Z \times B$ implies equicontinuity on B.

(b) This is Theorem 10.6 of Rockafellar (1970).

(c) This follows from part (b). Let C be any bounded, open, convex set containing the convex hull of B. Let $|\ \ |$ be the Euclidean norm. As defined, $s(*, *)$ is not necessarily bounded on $Z \times C$. But consider the sign-equivalent function

$$
\begin{aligned}
s_0(\zeta, c) &= [x(\zeta)'c]/|x(\zeta)| && \text{if } |x(\zeta)| > 0 \\
&= \quad\quad 0 && \text{if } x(\zeta) = 0
\end{aligned}
$$

By the Cauchy–Schwarz inequality, $s_0(\zeta, c) \leqslant |c|$. Boundedness of C then implies that $s_0(*, *)$ is bounded on $Z \times C$. For each $\zeta \in Z$, $s_0(\zeta, *)$ is linear on C, hence convex.   Q.E.D

7.3.5 The boundary assumption

Lemma 8 shows that Condition 9 is satisfied if $s(*, *)$ is linear on B and if certain conditional probability measures have bounded Lebesgue densities. This result suffices to cover the median-independent binary response model cited at the beginning of the chapter. It also covers linear versions of the median-independent separable model cited there. Note that part (c) of Lemma 7 has already verified that Condition 8b is satisfied for these models.

Lemma 8
Let $x(*)$ map Z into $X \subset R^K$. Let $v(*) \equiv [v_0(*), v_1(*)]$ and let V denote the range space of $v(*)$. Assume that

(i) Condition 8a holds with $s(\zeta, c) = x(\zeta)'c$.

(ii) For each c in B and each ω in V, the probability measure of $x'c$ conditional on the event $[v = \omega]$ is absolutely continuous with respect to Lebesgue measure μ. Moreover, there exists a $\lambda < \infty$ such that $\varphi_\mu(\eta, P_{x'c}|\omega) < \lambda$ for all $\eta \in R^1$ and $\omega \in V$.

(iii) The integrals $\int |v_0(z)| \, dP$ and $\int |v_1(z)| \, dP$ exist.

Then Condition 9 is satisfied. ■

PROOF It is enough to prove that the condition involving $v_0(*)$ holds.

For each $c \in B$ and $\alpha > 0$,

$$
\int_{Z_{c\alpha}} |v_0(z)| \, dP = \int 1[-\alpha < x(z)'c < \alpha] |v_0(z)| \, dP
$$

$$
= \int \left[\int_{-\alpha}^{\alpha} dP_{x'c}|v \right] |v_0| \, dP_v
$$

$$= \int \left[\int_{-\alpha}^{\alpha} \varphi_\mu(\eta, P_{x'c} | v) \, \mathrm{d}\mu \right] |v_0| \, \mathrm{d}P_v$$

$$\leqslant \int \left[\int_{-\alpha}^{\alpha} \lambda \, \mathrm{d}\mu \right] |v_0| \, \mathrm{d}P_v$$

$$= 2\alpha\lambda \int |v_0| \, \mathrm{d}P_v$$

Hence,

$$\sup_{c \in B} \int_{Z_{c\alpha}} |v_0(z)| \, \mathrm{d}P \leqslant 2\alpha\lambda \int |v_0| \, \mathrm{d}P_v$$

Letting $\alpha \to 0$ completes the proof.   Q.E.D.

CHAPTER 8

Limiting distributions in differentiable problems

Let b_N, $N = 1, \ldots, \infty$ be a sequence of point estimates of a parameter b solving a moment problem. (Where the estimate is set-valued, b_N is any element thereof.) This chapter gives conditions under which $\sqrt{N}(b_N - b)$ converges in distribution to a normal random variable.

The knowledge that normalized sequences of estimates have limiting normal distributions has at least two applications. First, it rationalizes use in large samples of the classical theory of hypothesis tests and confidence regions for normally distributed random variables. Second, it suggests a criterion for assessing the relative efficiency of alternative estimators, namely by comparison of the variances of their limiting normal distributions.

Asymptotic normality theorems are sometimes used in a third way. They are interpreted informally as making statements about the sampling behavior of the estimate b_N. In particular, it is sometimes said that in large samples, the sampling distribution of b_N is approximately normal with mean b and variance $V(1/N)$, where V is the variance of the limiting normal distribution of $\sqrt{N}(b_N - b)$. See, for example, Serfling (1980). This practice does not seem to have a formal justification and will not be followed here.

The analysis of this chapter is restricted to 'differentiable' moment problems. A moment equation is said to be differentiable if, for each ζ in Z, $g(\zeta, *)$ is continuously differentiable on B. A moment extremum problem is called differentiable if the functions $h(\zeta, *)$, $\zeta \in Z$ are twice continuously differentiable on B. Thus, differentiable moment problems are a subclass of the continuous problems treated in Chapter 7. Limiting distributions for some non-differentiable moment problems will receive attention in Chapter 9.

8.1 Linear moment equations

We begin by proving asymptotic normality for estimates of the parameter b solving a linear moment equation

$$\int [g_0(z) + g_1(z)b]\, \mathrm{d}P = 0 \tag{8.1}$$

Here $g_0(*)$ and $g_1(*)$ map Z into R^J and $R^{J \times K}$; $g_1(*)$ is written as a $J \times K$ matrix. The parameter space is $B = R^K$. So b solves the system of J linear equations in K unknowns

$$\Gamma + \Omega b = 0 \tag{8.2}$$

where $\Gamma \equiv \int g_0(z)\, \mathrm{d}P$ and $\Omega \equiv \int g_1(z)\, \mathrm{d}P$. It follows that b is identified if and only if the $J \times K$ matrix Ω has rank K.

We consider estimates obtained by letting the origin-preserving transformation $r(*)$ be a quadratic form

$$r(T) \equiv T'\Delta T \tag{8.3}$$

where Δ is a given $J \times J$ symmetric positive definite matrix. Let $\Gamma_N \equiv \int g_0(z)\, \mathrm{d}P_N$ and $\Omega_N \equiv \int g_1(z)\, \mathrm{d}P_N$. Then the method of moments estimate is

$$B_{N\Delta} \equiv \operatorname*{argmin}_{c \in B} [\Gamma_N + \Omega_N c]'\Delta[\Gamma_N + \Omega_N c] \tag{8.4}$$

The estimate $B_{N\Delta}$ always exists. In particular, $b_N \in B_{N\Delta}$ if and only if b_N solves the first-order condition

$$\Omega'_N \Delta \Gamma_N + (\Omega'_N \Delta \Omega_N)b_N = 0 \tag{8.5}$$

B_N is point-valued if and only if $\Omega'_N \Delta \Omega_N$ has rank K.

Quadratic form estimation of parameters solving linear moment equations is simple to analyze and has important applications. It is also central to an understanding of more complex asymptotic normality proofs. We shall see later that the key step in showing asymptotic normality in more general settings is to prove that, in large samples, the problem of interest can be well approximated by one of the class considered here. This done, asymptotic normality follows more or less immediately from the present analysis.

Theorem 1 gives conditions for the asymptotic normality of $\sqrt{N}(b_N - b)$.

Theorem 1
Let b solve (8.1) with $B = R^K$. Assume that Ω has rank K. Assume that

$\Sigma \equiv \int [g_0(z) + g_1(z)b][g_0(z) + g_1(z)b]' \, dP$ exists and has rank J. Assume that the observations z_i, $i = 1, \ldots, \infty$ are independent realizations from P. Let $b_N \in B_{N\Delta}$, $N = 1, \ldots, \infty$, where $B_{N\Delta}$ is as in (8.4). Then

$$\sqrt{N}(b_N - b) \xrightarrow{L} \mathbf{N}[0, (\Omega'\Delta\Omega)^{-1}(\Omega'\Delta\Sigma\Delta\Omega)(\Omega'\Delta\Omega)^{-1}] \qquad (8.6)$$

where $\xrightarrow{L}$ means 'convergence in law'. ∎

PROOF The assumption that Ω has rank K and the positive definiteness of Δ imply that the $K \times K$ matrix $\Omega'\Delta\Omega$ is non-singular. The random sampling assumption implies, by the strong law of large numbers, that as $N \to \infty$,

$$\Omega_N \to \Omega, \quad \text{a.s.} \qquad (8.7)$$

It follows from (8.7) and the continuity of $\Omega'\Delta\Omega$ as a function of Ω that

$$\Omega_N'\Delta\Omega_N \to \Omega'\Delta\Omega, \quad \text{a.s.} \qquad (8.8)$$

It follows from (8.8) and the continuity of the matrix inverse transformation that there almost surely exists a finite sample size N_0 such that $\Omega_N'\Delta\Omega_N$ is non-singular for $N > N_0$. Therefore, for $N > N_0$, (8.5) has the unique solution

$$b_N = -(\Omega_N'\Delta\Omega_N)^{-1}\Omega_N'\Delta\Gamma_N \qquad (8.9)$$

For $N > N_0$, the identity

$$b \equiv (\Omega_N'\Delta\Omega_N)^{-1}(\Delta_N'\Delta\Omega_N)b \qquad (8.10)$$

holds. It follows from (8.9) and (8.10) that for $N > N_0$,

$$\sqrt{N}(b_N - b) = -(\Omega_N'\Delta\Omega_N)^{-1}\Omega_N'\Delta[\sqrt{N}(\Gamma_N + \Omega_N b)] \qquad (8.11)$$

The expression $\Gamma_N + \Omega_N b$ is the sample average of $g_0(z) + g_1(z)b$. By (8.1), $g_0(z) + g_1(z)b$ has mean zero. By assumption, $g_0(z) + g_1(z)b$ has positive definite variance matrix Σ. Hence, the assumption of random sampling implies, by the multivariate Lindberg–Levy central limit theorem (see Rao, 1973, pp. 127–9),

$$\sqrt{N}[\Gamma_N + \Omega_N b] \xrightarrow{L} \mathbf{N}(0, \Sigma) \qquad (8.12)$$

The theorem now follows from (8.7), (8.8), (8.11), and (8.12).

Q.E.D.

8.1.1 *Strong consistency of* b_N

Theorem 1 implicitly proves that b_N is a weakly consistent estimate for b. If $\sqrt{N}(b_N - b)$ has any limiting distribution, then $b_N - b$ necessarily converges in probability to zero.

In fact, b_N is strongly consistent. To see this, consider $N > N_0$. By (8.11),

$$b_N - b = -(\Omega_N'\Delta\Omega_N)^{-1}\Omega_N'\Delta(\Gamma_N + \Omega_N b) \tag{8.13}$$

Now let $N \to \infty$. By the strong law of large numbers,

$$(\Omega_N'\Delta\Omega_N)^{-1}\Omega_N'\Delta \to (\Omega'\Delta\Omega)^{-1}\Omega'\Delta, \quad \text{a.s.} \tag{8.14}$$

and

$$\Gamma_N + \Omega_N b \to \Gamma + \Omega b = 0, \quad \text{a.s.} \tag{8.15}$$

It follows that

$$b_N \to b, \quad \text{a.s.} \tag{8.16}$$

Note that this consistency result does not require that the variance matrix Σ exist. In contrast to the analysis of Chapter 7, the present finding does not assume a compact parameter space.

8.1.2 *The case* $J = K$

When the number of moment equations J equals the number of parameters K, the sample moment equation $\Gamma_N + \Omega_N b_N = 0$ is a system of K equations in K unknowns and so always has a solution. Hence, the method of moments estimate is the same for all choices of $r(*)$. Let the assumptions of Theorem 1 hold. Then it follows from (8.9) that

$$b_N = -(\Omega_N)^{-1}\Gamma_N \tag{8.17}$$

for $N > N_0$. The conclusion to Theorem 1 reduces to

$$\sqrt{N}(b_N - b) \xrightarrow{L} N(0, \Omega^{-1}\Sigma\Omega'^{-1}) \tag{8.18}$$

When $J > K$, the method of moment estimate varies with $r(*)$. Within the class of quadratic form functions, the selected matrix Δ affects the estimate's value and the variance of its limiting normal distribution. It is natural to ask how one should choose Δ. This question will be treated in Section 8.2.

Note that in no case does the variance of the limiting distribution depend on the value of Γ.

8.1.3 *Instrumental variables models*

Let us apply Theorem 1 to obtain the limiting distribution of the Wright–Reiersol instrumental variables estimate, discussed in Section 2.5. Here $v(*)$ and $x(*)$ map Z into R^K, $y(*)$ maps Z into R^1, and b solves the linear moment equation

$$\int v(z)[y(z) - x(z)'b]\,dP = 0 \qquad (8.19)$$

So $g_0(*) \equiv v(*)y(*)$, $g_1(*) \equiv -v(*)x(*)'$ and $J = K$. Equation (8.17) implies that for $N > N_0$,

$$b_N = \left[\int vx'\,dP_{Nvx} \right]^{-1} \left[\int vy\,dP_{Nvy} \right] \qquad (8.20)$$

The limiting distribution of $\sqrt{N}(b_N - b)$ is normal with mean zero and variance

$$\Omega^{-1}\Sigma\Omega'^{-1} = \left[\int vx'\,dP_{vx} \right]^{-1} \left[\int \{y - x'b\}^2 vv'\,dP_{vyx} \right]$$
$$\times \left[\int xv'\,dP_{vx} \right]^{-1} \qquad (8.21)$$

Consider the special case in which $v(*) = x(*)$. Then b_N is the least squares estimate

$$b_N = \left[\int xx'\,dP_{Nx} \right]^{-1} \left[\int xy\,dP_{Nxy} \right] \qquad (8.22)$$

The variance of the limiting distribution is

$$\Omega^{-1}\Sigma\Omega'^{-1} = \left[\int xx'\,dP \right]^{-1} \left[\int \lambda(x)xx'\,dP_x \right] \left[\int xx'\,dP_x \right]^{-1} \qquad (8.23)$$

where $\lambda(\xi) \equiv \int(y - \xi b)^2\,dP_y|\xi,\ \xi \in X$.

It is of interest to compare (8.23) with the familiar least squares asymptotic variance expression $\sigma^2[\int xx'\,dP_x]^{-1}$, where σ^2 is the unconditional variance of $(y - xb)$. The variance expression in (8.23) reduces to the familiar one if xb is the mean regression of y on x and if y is variance independent of x. Then $\lambda(\xi) = \sigma^2$, $\xi \in X$.

8.2   Differentiable moment equations

Theorem 2 of Chapter 7 gave conditions which imply the consistency of method of moments estimates in continuous moment equations. We shall show here that such estimates are asymptotically normal, provided that the regularity assumed in the consistency theorem is strengthened. In what follows, the assumptions employed in Chapter 7 are labeled Conditions 7.1 through 7.9 to distinguish them from the new assumptions to be introduced below. The same convention is applied to the theorems and lemmas of Chapter 7.

The theorem to be presented here retains the essential assumption that the parameter b is identified (Condition 7.1a). It retains the assumption of random sampling (Condition 7.7). It replaces the other conditions of the consistency theorem with the following stronger assumptions.

Condition 1 (Origin-preserving transformation)
(a) $r(*)$ is twice continuously differentiable and $r(0) = 0$.
(b) For each $\varepsilon > 0$, $\inf\limits_{|T| > \varepsilon} r(T) > 0$.
(c) The $J \times J$ matrix $\Delta \equiv \partial^2 r(0)/\partial T \partial T'$ is positive definite.

Condition 2 (Differentiability)
(a) For each $\zeta \in Z$, $g(\zeta, *)$ is continuously differentiable on B.
(b) The $J \times K$ matrix $\Omega \equiv \int [\partial g(z, b)/\partial a'] \, dP$ exists and has rank K.

Condition 3 (Boundedness)
(a) There exists a function $D_0(*)$ mapping Z into $[0, \infty)$ such that

    (i) The integral $\int D_0(z) \, dP$ exists and is finite.
    (ii) $|g(\zeta, c)| \leqslant D_0(\zeta)$ for all (ζ, c) in $Z \times B$.
(b) There exists a function $D_1(*)$ mapping Z into $[0, \infty)$ such that

    (i) The integral $\int D_1(z) \, dP$ exists and is finite.
    (ii) $|\partial g(\zeta, c)/\partial a'| \leqslant D_1(\zeta)$ for all (ζ, c) in $Z \times B$.

Condition 4 (Variance)
The $J \times J$ matrix $\Sigma = \int g(z, b)g(z, b)' \, dP$ exists and is positive definite.

Condition 5 (Parameter space)
(a) The parameter space B is compact.
(b) $b \in B_0 \subset B$ for some open set B_0.

We now prove Theorem 2. Discussion follows.

Theorem 2
Assume that Conditions 7.1a, 7.7, and 1, 2, 3, 4, and 5 above hold.
Then B_{Nr} is non-empty for all N. Let $b_N \in B_{Nr}$, $N = 1, \ldots, \infty$. Then

$$\sqrt{N}(b_N - b) \overset{L}{\longrightarrow} N[0, (\Omega'\Delta\Omega)^{-1}(\Omega'\Delta\Sigma\Delta\Omega)(\Omega'\Delta\Omega)^{-1}] \quad \blacksquare \quad (8.24)$$

PROOF   The proof has three steps. First we show that the sequence
of estimates $\{b_N\}$ exists and converges almost surely to b. Next we
prove that, in large samples, $\sqrt{N}(b_N - b)$ behaves like a linear
function of $\sqrt{N}\int g(z, b)\,dP_N$. This step is the most lengthy. Third, we
cite the fact that $\sqrt{N}\int g(z, b)\,dP_N$ has a limiting normal distribution.
The theorem then follows from the fact that linear functions of normal
random variables are normally distributed.

Step 1:   By Conditions 1a, 2a, and 5a, $r[\int g(z, *)\,dP_N]$ is a continuous
function on the compact set B and so attains its infimum. Hence B_{Nr}
exists. Conditions 1, 2, 3, and 5 respectively imply Conditions 7.3, 7.4,
7.5, and 7.6. Hence B_{Nr} is strongly consistent by Theorem 7.2.

Step 2:   Given consistency, there almost surely exists an N_0 such that
$b_N \in B_0$ for $N > N_0$. Conditions 1a and 2a imply that for $N > N_0$, b_N
satisfies the first-order condition

$$\frac{\partial r\left[\int g(z, b_N)\,dP_N\right]}{\partial a} = \left[\int \frac{\partial g(z, b_N)}{\partial a'}\,dP_N\right]'\left[\frac{\partial r\left[\int g(z, b_N)\,dP_N\right]}{\partial T}\right] = 0$$
$$(8.25)$$

By Condition 1a and the mean value theorem, there are points
$T_{Nj} \in R^J, j = 1, \ldots, J$, each on the line segment connecting $\int g(z, b_N)\,dP_N$
and zero, such that for each $j = 1, \ldots, J$,

$$\left[\frac{\partial r\left[\int g(z, b_N)\,dP_N\right]}{\partial T_j}\right] = \frac{\partial r(0)}{\partial T_j} + \left[\frac{\partial^2 r(T_{Nj})}{\partial T_j \partial T'}\right]\left[\int g(z, b_N)\,dP_N\right]$$
$$(8.26)$$

But $\partial r(0)/\partial T = 0$ by Condition 1. So (8.25) and (8.26) imply that

$$\left[\int \frac{\partial g(z, b_N)}{\partial a'}\,dP_N\right]'\left[\frac{\partial^2 r(T_N)}{\partial T \partial T'}\right]\left[\int g(z, b_N)\,dP_N\right] = 0 \quad (8.27)$$

where $T_N \equiv (T_{Nj}, j = 1, \ldots, J)$ and where we understand $r(T_N)$ to mean that the jth row of $\partial^2 r(T_N)/\partial T \partial T'$ is evaluated at T_{Nj}.

By Condition 2a and a second application of the mean value theorem, there exist points $c_{Nj} \in R^K$, $j = 1, \ldots, J$, each on the line segment connecting b_N and b, such that for each $j = 1, \ldots, J$,

$$\left[\int g_j(z, b_N) \, dP_N \right] = \left[\int g_j(z, b) \, dP_N \right]$$
$$+ \left[\int \frac{\partial g_j(z, c_{Nj})}{\partial a'} \, dP_N \right] (b_N - b) \qquad (8.28)$$

Inserting (8.28) into (8.27) gives

$$\left[\int \frac{\partial g(z, b_N)}{\partial a'} \, dP_N \right]' \left[\frac{\partial^2 r(T_N)}{\partial T \partial T'} \right] \left[\int g(z, b) \, dP_N \right]$$
$$+ \left[\int \frac{\partial g(z, b_N)}{\partial a'} \, dP_N \right]' \left[\frac{\partial^2 r(T_N)}{\partial T \partial T'} \right]$$
$$\times \left[\int \frac{\partial g(z, c_N)}{\partial a'} \, dP_N \right] (b_N - b) = 0 \qquad (8.29)$$

where $c_N \equiv (c_{Nj}, j = 1, \ldots, J)$ and where we understand $g(z, c_N)$ to mean that the jth row of $\partial g(z, c_N)/\partial a'$ is evaluated at c_{Nj}.

Now let $N \to \infty$. Conditions 7.7, 2a, 3, and 5a imply, by the uniform law of large numbers of Lemma 7.3, that

$$\sup_{c \in B} \left| \int g(z, c) \, dP_N - \int g(z, c) \, dP \right| \to 0, \quad \text{a.s.}$$

and

$$\sup_{c \in B} \left| \int [\partial g(z, c)/\partial a'] \, dP_N - \int [\partial g(z, c)/\partial a] \, dP \right| \to 0, \quad \text{a.s.}$$

It follows from this and from the consistency of b_N that

$$\int \frac{\partial g(z, b_N)}{\partial a'} \, dP_N \to \Omega, \quad \text{a.s.} \qquad (8.30)$$

$$\frac{\partial^2 r(T_N)}{\partial T \partial T'} \to \Delta, \quad \text{a.s.} \qquad (8.31)$$

and

$$\int \frac{\partial g(z, c_N)}{\partial a'} \, dP_N \to \Omega, \quad \text{a.s.} \qquad (8.32)$$

By Conditions 1c and 2b, $\Omega'\Delta\Omega$ is non-singular. It follows from this and from (8.29) that there almost surely exists a finite $N_1 > N_0$ such that

$$\sqrt{N}(b_N - b) = -\left[\left[\int \frac{\partial g(z, b_N)'}{\partial a} dP_N\right]\left[\frac{\partial^2 r(T_N)}{\partial T \partial T'}\right]\right.$$

$$\times \left[\int \frac{\partial g(z, c_N)}{\partial a'} dP_N\right]\right]^{-1}\left[\int \frac{\partial g(z, b_N)'}{\partial a} dP_N\right]$$

$$\times \left[\frac{\partial^2 r(T_N)}{\partial T \partial T'}\right]\left[\sqrt{N}\int g(z, b) dP_N\right] \qquad (8.33)$$

for $N > N_1$. Given (8.30), (8.31), and (8.32), this shows that $\sqrt{N}(b_N - b)$ is asymptotically a linear function of $\sqrt{N}\int g(z, b) dP_N$.

Step 3: By condition 7.1a and Condition 4, $g(z, b)$ has mean zero and positive definite variance Σ. Therefore, Condition 7.7 and the Lindberg–Levy central limit theorem imply that

$$\sqrt{N}\left[\int g(z, b) dP_N\right] \xrightarrow{L} \mathbf{N}(0, \Sigma) \qquad (8.34)$$

Combining (8.30) through (8.34) proves the theorem.   Q.E.D.

8.2.1 *Discussion*

Of the conditions imposed by Theorem 2, some are basic. Identification and the condition defining an origin-preserving transformation (Condition 1a) are obviously essential. The assumption that b is interior to B (Condition 5b) also seems necessary. If b were on the boundary of B, the estimate b_N would always lie to one side of b, no matter how large N is. Then $\sqrt{N}(b_N - b)$ could not have a limiting normal distribution.

The critical function of the matrix rank Conditions 1c and 2b is to ensure that $\Omega'\Delta\Omega$ is non-singular. Whatever the rank of $\Omega'\Delta\Omega$, (8.29), (8.30), (8.31), (8.32), and (8.34) imply that as $N \to \infty$,

$$\Omega'\Delta\Omega[\sqrt{N}(b_N - b)] \xrightarrow{L} \mathbf{N}(0, \Omega'\Delta\Sigma\Delta\Omega) \qquad (8.35)$$

Thus, certain linear functions of $\sqrt{N}(b_N - b)$ have limiting normal distributions even if $\Omega'\Delta\Omega$ is singular. But non-singularity is required for $\sqrt{N}(b_N - b)$ itself to have a limiting distribution.

Some of the conditions of Theorem 2 can be weakened or modified without negating the theorem's conclusion. Our treatment of linear moment problems in Section 8.1 demonstrated that compactness of B (Condition 5a) can be eliminated if $g(*, *)$ is sufficiently well-behaved. The differentiability Conditions 1a and 2a impose more smoothness on $r(*)$ and on $g(\zeta, *)$, $\zeta \in Z$ than necessary. Assuming that the consistency of b_N has somehow been shown, the remainder of the proof of Theorem 2 remains valid if these conditions hold only in neighborhoods of zero and b respectively.

Similarly, the random sampling assumption is convenient but not essential. Versions of Theorem 2 can be proved for other sampling processes regular enough to yield a law of large numbers and central limit theorem. The one aspect of Theorem 2 that is specific to random sampling is the result that $\sqrt{N} \int g(z, b) \, dP_N$ has asymptotic variance Σ. For other sampling processes, the asymptotic variance may differ from Σ.

The remainder of this section examines the manner in which one's choice of an origin-preserving transformation $r(*)$ affects the limiting distribution of $\sqrt{N}(b_N - b)$.

8.2.2 The case $J = K$

When the number of equations J equals the number of parameters K, (8.33) reduces to

$$\sqrt{N}(b_N - b) = - \left[\int \frac{\partial g(z, c_N)}{\partial a'} \, dP_N \right]^{-1} \left[\sqrt{N} \int g(z, b) \, dP_N \right] \tag{8.36}$$

Let $r_1(*)$ and $r_2(*)$ be any two functions satisfying Condition 1 and let b_{N1} and b_{N2} be corresponding estimates of b. The value of c_N in (8.36) depends on b_N, which may depend on $r(*)$. So (8.36) does not imply that the estimates b_{N1} and b_{N2} are the same. But it does follow from (8.32), (8.34), and (8.36) that

$$\sqrt{N}(b_{N1} - b_{N2}) \xrightarrow{P} 0 \tag{8.37}$$

where $\xrightarrow{P}$ means 'convergence in probability'. Thus, all choices of $r(*)$ that satisfy Condition 1 yield estimates that are asymptotically equivalent to order $\sqrt{N}$.

The result (8.37) is an asymptotic version of the result reported in

Section 8.1 for problems where $\int g(z, *) dP_N$ is a linear function on $B = R^K$. There, $J = K$ implied that the sample moment equation always has a solution. So the analog estimate was the same for all choices of $r(*)$. If $g(*, *)$ is nonlinear on B or if B is a proper subset of R^K, having $J = K$ does not guarantee that the sample moment equation has a solution. So the chosen $r(*)$ may affect the value of the estimate. What (8.37) shows is that to order $\sqrt{N}$, the effect of $r(*)$ on estimation is negligible.

When $J = K$, the variance of the common limiting distribution for all $r(*)$ satisfying Condition 1 reduces from the expression given in (8.24) to a simpler one not involving Δ. The following corollary to Theorem 2 states the result.

Corollary 1
Assume that the conditions of Theorem 2 hold and that $J = K$. Then

$$\sqrt{N}(b_N - b) \xrightarrow{L} N(0, \Omega^{-1}\Sigma\Omega'^{-1}) \quad \blacksquare \qquad (8.38)$$

8.2.3 *Asymptotic equivalence classes of r(*) when J > K*

Now consider the case $J < K$. Let $r_1(*)$ and $r_2(*)$ be any two functions satisfying Condition 1 and the condition $\Delta_1 \equiv \partial^2 r_1(0)/\partial T \partial T' = \partial^2 r_2(0)/\partial T \partial T' \equiv \Delta_2$. Let b_{N1} and b_{N2} be corresponding estimates of b. In general, equality of Δ_1 and Δ_2 does not imply equality of b_{N1} and b_{N2}. But it does follows from (8.30) through (8.34) that

$$\sqrt{N}(b_{N1} - b_{N2}) \xrightarrow{P} 0 \qquad (8.39)$$

Thus, all choices of $r(*)$ that satisfy Condition 1 and have the same second derivative evaluated at zero yield estimates that are asymptotically equivalent to order $\sqrt{N}$.

This result provides a statistical rationale for a common practice. For computational reasons, applied researchers often use a quadratic form transformation of the moment equation, that is one where $r(T) = T'\Delta T$ for given Δ. Equation (8.39) shows that from the perspective of first-order asymptotic theory, restriction of attention to such $r(*)$ is innocuous.

Simply observe that Δ is the second derivative matrix of $T'\Delta T$. Let $r_1(*)$ be any function satisfying Condition 1. It follows from (8.39) that estimation using the quadratic form function $r_2(T) =$

$T'[\partial^2 r_1(0)/\partial T \partial T']T$ is asymptotically equivalent to order $\sqrt{N}$ to estimation using $r_1(*)$.

8.2.4 Asymptotic best Δ when $J > K$

When $J > K$, the variance of the limiting distribution of $\sqrt{N}(b_N - b)$ is $(\Omega'\Delta\Omega)^{-1}(\Omega'\Delta\Sigma\Delta\Omega)(\Omega'\Delta\Omega)^{-1}$. So functions $r(*)$ with different values of Δ generally imply limiting distributions with different variances. The following result reported in Hansen (1982, Theorem 3.2) provides the value of Δ that minimizes asymptotic variance in the matrix sense.

Corollary 2
Assume that the conditions of Theorem 2 hold. Then

$$\sqrt{N}(b_N - b) \xrightarrow{L} N[0, (\Omega'\Sigma^{-1}\Omega)^{-1} + DD'] \qquad (8.40)$$

where $D \equiv (\Omega'\Delta\Omega)^{-1}\Omega'\Delta W - (\Omega'\Sigma^{-1}\Omega)^{-1}\Omega'W'^{-1}$ and where W is any non-singular $J \times J$ matrix such that $\Sigma = WW'$. If $\Delta = \Sigma^{-1}$, then $D = 0$. ∎

PROOF Evaluation of the expression DD' verifies that the variance matrix in (8.40) is the same as that in (8.24). Evaluation of D for the case $\Delta = \Sigma^{-1}$ yields the result $D = 0$. Q.E.D.

Thus, the variance of the limiting normal distribution of $\sqrt{N}(b_N - b)$ exceeds $(\Omega'\Sigma^{-1}\Omega)^{-1}$ by a non-negative definite matrix that depends on Δ. Setting $\Delta = \Sigma^{-1}$ makes the variance attain the lower bound.

The matrix Σ is not known so the ideal estimate is not computable. On the other hand, a multi-step procedure yields a computable estimate that can be shown asymptotically equivalent to the ideal (Hansen, 1982). Select some positive definite $J \times J$ matrix Δ_0 and compute

$$B_{N0} \equiv \operatorname*{argmin}_{c \in B} \left[\int g(z, c) \, dP_N \right]' \Delta_0 \left[\int g(z, c) \, dP_N \right] \qquad (8.41)$$

Pick a point $b_{N0} \in B_{N0}$ and compute

$$\Sigma_N \equiv \int g(z, b_{N0}) g(z, b_{N0})' \, dP_N \qquad (8.42)$$

Now re-estimate b by

$$B_{N1} \equiv \operatorname*{argmin}_{c \in B} \left[\int g(z,c) \, dP_N \right]' \Sigma_N^{-1} \left[\int g(z,c) \, dP_N \right] \quad (8.43)$$

The above derivation of B_{N1} applies the analogy principle recursively, first to obtain b_{N0}, then Σ_N, and finally B_{N1}. This recursion can be rewritten, albeit somewhat clumsily, as a single application of the analogy principle. B_{N1} minimizes on B the sample analog of the following origin-preserving transformation of the moment equation:

$$\left[\int g(z,b) \, dP \right]' \omega(P)^{-1} \left[\int g(z,b) \, dP \right] = 0 \quad (8.44)$$

where $\omega(P) \equiv \int [g\{z,c(P)\}][g\{z,c(P)\}]' \, dP$ and where

$$c(P) \in \operatorname*{argmin}_{c \in B} \left[\int g(z,c) \, dP \right]' \Delta_0 \left[\int g(z,c) \, dP \right] \quad (8.45)$$

Simply observe that $c(P_N) = b_{N0}$ and $\omega(P_N) = \Sigma_N$.

8.2.5 *Asymptotic bound on precision of estimation*

Corollary 2 says that the limiting distribution of $\sqrt{N}(b_N - b)$ can have no smaller variance than $(\Omega'\Sigma^{-1}\Omega)^{-1}$. But this asymptotic bound on precision applies only to method of moments estimates. It leaves open the possibility that there exists some other procedure which estimates b more precisely.

Chamberlain (1987) shows that if b is known to solve a differentiable moment equation and no other information about b is available, then in a certain sense no estimate of b can be more precise than the best method of moments estimate. In particular, an 'asymptotic minimax' theorem of the Hajek (1972) type holds. Formal statement of asymptotic minimax theorems is somewhat involved. We shall suffice with a brief discussion.

Asymptotic minimax theorems interpret the task of choosing an estimate of a parameter as a problem of selecting a best predictor. Let b denote a finite-dimensional parameter solving a problem $T(P,b) = 0$. Let b_N be a point predictor (estimate) of b based on a sample of size N. Let $L(*)$ be any symmetric loss function mapping values of $\sqrt{N}(b_N - b)$ into $[0, \infty)$. Hajek began by seeking a predictor b_N that minimizes asymptotic expected loss with respect to the sampling distribution of $\sqrt{N(b_N - b)}$. The solution to this problem, however, depends on the unknown value of b. So he reformulated the objective to be selection of a minimax predictor, that is one that minimizes the maximum expected loss over all the possible values of the parameter.

Chamberlain applies the Hajek approach to the problem of choosing a predictor of a parameter solving a differentiable moment equation. He shows that the asymptotic maximum expected loss of any predictor is at least as large as the maximum expected loss that occurs for a predictor with the limiting distribution $N[0, (\Omega' \Sigma^{-1} \Omega)^{-1}]$. See Section 9.1 for details.

8.3   Differentiable moment extremum problems

Asymptotic normality of method of moments estimates in differentiable extremum problems is a direct consequence of Theorem 2.

Theorem 2′
Assume the conditions of Theorem 7.2′. Assume that

$$g(\zeta, c) \equiv \partial h(\zeta, c)/\partial a, \qquad (\zeta, c) \in Z \times B \tag{8.46}$$

exists and satisfies Conditions 2, 3, and 4. Also assume Condition 5. Let $b_N \in B_N$, $N = 1, \ldots, \infty$. Then

$$\sqrt{N(b_N - b)} \xrightarrow{L} N(0, \Omega^{-1} \Sigma \Omega'^{-1}) \tag{8.47}$$

where

$$\Omega \equiv \int [\partial g(z, b)/\partial a'] dP = \int [\partial^2 h(z, b)/\partial a \partial a'] dP \tag{8.48}$$

and

$$\Sigma \equiv \int g(z, b)g(z, b)' dP$$

$$= \int [\partial h(z, b)/\partial a] [\partial h(z, b)/\partial a'] dP \quad \blacksquare \tag{8.49}$$

PROOF   By assumption, b solves the extremum problem

$$b - \operatorname*{argmin}_{c \in B} \int h(z, c) dP = 0 \tag{8.50}$$

and is an element of B_0, an open set within B. The Lebesgue bounded convergence theorem implies that the moment function $\int h(z, *)dP$ is differentiable on B_0 with

$$\partial\left[\int h(z, *)dP\right]\bigg/\partial a = \int [\partial h(z, *)/\partial a]dP \qquad (8.51)$$

(The argument is the same as that applied in Lemma 7.2 to show that $\int g(z, *)dP$ is continuous on B.) It follows that b solves the first-order condition

$$\partial\left[\int h(z, b)dP\right]\bigg/\partial a = \int [\partial h(z, b)/\partial a]dP = 0 \qquad (8.52)$$

This is a K-variate moment equation in a K-dimensional parameter.

Consider the method of moments estimate

$$B_N \equiv \underset{c \in B}{\operatorname{argmin}} \int h(z, c)dP_N \qquad (8.53)$$

Let $b_N \in B_N$. Strong consistency of B_N (Theorem 7.2′) implies that there almost surely exists a finite sample size N_0 such that $B_N \subset B_0$ for $N > N_0$. It follows that for $N > N_0$, b_N solves the first-order condition

$$\int [\partial h(z, b_N)/\partial a]dP_N = 0 \qquad (8.54)$$

Equation (8.54) is the sample analog of the moment equation (8.52). Hence, Steps 2 and 3 of the proof to Theorem 2 may be applied to obtain the limiting distribution of $\sqrt{N}(b_N - b)$. Corollary 1 shows that the limiting normal distribution is as given in (8.47).   Q.E.D.

8.3.1 *An extremum problem and its first-order condition*

The parameter b solves both the moment extremum problem (8.50) and the moment equation (8.52). Let $C \subset B$ denote the set of solutions to (8.52). The proof to Theorem 2′ showed that b is an element of C. This proof does not guarantee that C contains only the point b. It may be that the extremum problem identifies b but that its first-order condition does not.

The analogy principle may be applied either to (8.50) or to (8.52). Let C_N be the method of moments estimate based on (8.52). The proof to Theorem 2′ showed that $B_N \subset C_N$ for $N > N_0$. The estimate C_N may contain points not in B_N; this will generally be the case if (8.52) does not identify b. So estimation based on (8.50) is preferable to estimation based on (8.52).

8.4 Differentiable conditional likelihood problems

The foregoing analysis of limiting distributions of method of moments estimates takes the specification of the finite-dimensional moment problem as given. Often, the available information implies that the parameter of interest solves infinitely many finite-dimensional problems. Section 2.1 noted that a parameter solving an index problem solves infinitely many moment equations. Section 4.3 showed that a best predictor solves infinitely many moment extremum problems. Section 6.1 showed that a mean-independent separable econometric model implies infinitely many orthogonality conditions.

One would like to characterize the best attainable precision of estimation in these settings. One would also like to know whether application of the analogy principle to some finite-dimensional moment problem solved by the parameter yields an efficient estimate. A major achievement of statistical theory has been to provide asymptotically valid answers to these questions for the class of differentiable, finite-dimensional likelihood problems. This section describes the findings. Chapter 9 will discuss recent research on efficient estimation of more general likelihood problems.

8.4.1 *The information bound*

Recall that in a likelihood problem, probability measure P is known to be a member of a family of probability measures $[\tau(c), c \in B]$, all of which are absolutely continuous with respect to some measure v on Z. A likelihood problem is finite dimensional if the parameter space B is a subset of R^K. A finite-dimensional likelihood problem is differentiable if the densities $\varphi_v(\zeta, *), \zeta \in Z$ are continuously differentiable on B.

Assume that the Fisher information matrix

$$\iota \equiv \int [\partial \log \varphi_v(z, b)/\partial a][\partial \log \varphi_v(z, b)/\partial a']\, dP \qquad (8.55)$$

exists and is non-singular. Let a random sample from P be drawn and let b_N, $N = 1, \ldots, \infty$ be a sequence of estimates of b. The 'information bound' states, in various formal senses, that $\sqrt{N}(b_N - b)$ cannot have a limiting distribution more concentrated around zero than is the $N(0, \iota^{-1})$ distribution.

Classical versions of the information bound are given in Cramer (1946) and Rao (1973). The Hajek (1972) asymptotic minimax theorem alluded to in Section 8.2 is one of two modern statements of the bound. The other is the Hajek (1970) 'representation theorem'. The representation theorem proves that if $\sqrt{N}(b_N - b)$ has limiting distribution $l(b)$ and if certain uniformity conditions hold, then $l(b)$ can be written as the distribution of the sum $\delta + \varepsilon$, where δ is an $N[0, \iota^{-1}]$ random variable and ε is independent of δ. For expositions of the various information bound theorems, see Ibragimov and Has'minskii (1981).

The information bound holds not only for likelihood problems but also for conditional likelihood problems. We shall present an information bound result for method of moments estimation based on a differentiable finite-dimensional moment equation.

Let b solve a differentiable conditional likelihood problem satisfying Condition 6 below. Let b be estimated by application of the analogy principle to an implied finite-dimensional moment equation satisfying Condition 7. Theorem 3 shows that the limiting normal distribution of $\sqrt{N}(b_N - b)$ has variance at least as large, in the matrix sense, as a conditional likelihood version of Fisher information.

The statements of Conditions 6 and 7 use the conditional likelihood notation developed in Chapter 5. Discussion of these conditions follows presentation of Theorem 3.

Condition 6 (Differentiable conditional likelihood)
(a) For $\xi \in X$, $P_y | \xi = \tau_\xi(b) \in [\tau_\xi(c), c \in B]$.
(b) For $\xi \in X$, there exists a measure ν_ξ on Y such that $\tau_\xi(c)$, $c \in B$ are dominated by ν_ξ. $\varphi_\xi(\eta, c) > 0$, $(\eta, \xi, c) \in Y \times X \times B$.
(c) For $(\xi, \eta) \in X \times Y$, $\varphi_\xi(\eta, *)$ is continuously differentiable on B.
(d) The Fisher information matrix

$$\iota \equiv \int [\partial \log \varphi_x(y, b)/\partial a] [\partial \log \varphi_x(y, b)/\partial a'] dP_{yx} \qquad (8.56)$$

is finite and non-singular.

Condition 7 (Moment problem)
(a) $g(\zeta, c) = g[\{y(\zeta), x(\zeta)\}, c]$, $(\zeta, c) \in Z \times B$.

(b) $\int g(y, \xi, c)\varphi_\xi(y, c)dv_\xi = 0$, $(\xi, c) \in X \times B$.
(c) For each $\xi \in X$, there exists a $D_\xi(*)$ mapping Y into $[0, \infty)$ such that

  (i) The integral $\int D_\xi(y)dv_\xi$ exists.
  (ii) $|\partial[g(\eta, \xi, c)\varphi_\xi(\eta, c)]/\partial a'| \leqslant D_\xi(\eta)$, $(\eta, c) \in Y \times B$.

Theorem 3
Assume the conditions of Theorem 2 and Conditions 6 and 7. Then

$$\sqrt{N}(b_N - b) \xrightarrow{L} \mathbf{N}(0, \iota^{-1} + E) \tag{8.57}$$

where E is a positive semidefinite $K \times K$ matrix.   ■

PROOF Fix $\xi \in X$. Condition 7b says that $\int g(y, \xi, *)\varphi_\xi(y, *)dv_\xi$ equals zero on B. Hence, $\int g(y, \xi, *)\varphi_\xi(y, *)dv_\xi$ is differentiable on B with derivative zero everywhere. By Condition 7c and the Lebesgue bounded convergence theorem,

$$0 = \frac{\partial \int g(y, \xi, b)\varphi_\xi(y, b)dv_\xi}{\partial a'}$$

$$= \int \frac{\partial[g(y, \xi, b)\varphi_\xi(y, b)]}{\partial a'}dv_\xi$$

$$= \int \frac{\partial g(y, \xi, b)}{\partial a'}\varphi_\xi(y, b)dv_\xi + \int g(y, \xi, b)\frac{\partial \varphi_\xi(y, b)}{\partial a'}dv_\xi$$

$$= \int \frac{\partial g(y, \xi, b)}{\partial a'}dP_y|\xi + \int g(y, \xi, b)\frac{\partial \log \varphi_\xi(y, b)}{\partial a'}dP_y|\xi \tag{8.58}$$

(The argument is again the same as was applied in Lemma 7.2 to show that $\int g(z, *)dP$ is continuous on B.)

Taking the expectation of (8.58) with respect to P_x, we find that

$$\Omega \equiv \int \frac{\partial g(y, x, b)}{\partial a'}dP_{yx}$$

$$= -\int g(y, x, b)\frac{\partial \log \varphi_x(y, b)}{\partial a'}dP_{yx} \tag{8.59}$$

where Ω was defined in Condition 2. The equality (8.59) has previously been applied for other purposes in Tauchen (1985) and Newey (1985).

By Corollary 2 to Theorem 2, the variance of the limiting distribution of $\sqrt{N}(b_N - b)$ is bounded from below by $(\Omega'\Sigma^{-1}\Omega)^{-1}$. But

$$(\Omega'\Sigma^{-1}\Omega)^{-1} = \iota^{-1} + E \tag{8.60}$$

where E is a positive semidefinite matrix. To see this, consider the $(K + J) \times (K + J)$ matrix

$$\begin{bmatrix} \iota & -\Omega' \\ -\Omega & \Sigma \end{bmatrix}$$

$$= \begin{bmatrix} \int \dfrac{\partial \log \varphi_x(y, b)}{\partial a} \dfrac{\partial \log \varphi_x(y, b)}{\partial a'} dP_{yx} & \int \dfrac{\partial \log \varphi_x(y, b)}{\partial a} g(y, x, b)' dP_{yx} \\ \int g(y, x, b) \dfrac{\partial \log \varphi_x(y, b)}{\partial a'} dP_{yx} & \int g(y, x, b) g(y, x, b)' dP_{yx} \end{bmatrix}$$

$$\tag{8.61}$$

The matrix (8.61) is positive semidefinite; hence $\iota - \Omega'\Sigma^{-1}\Omega$ is positive semidefinite. It follows that $(\Omega'\Sigma^{-1}\Omega)^{-1} - \iota^{-1}$ is positive semidefinite.   Q.E.D.

8.4.2 *The conditional likelihood assumption*

Conditions 6a and 6b define a conditional likelihood problem. Note that Condition 6b assumes everywhere positive densities. The proof to Theorem 3 can be extended to allow regions of zero density, provided that these regions do not vary on the parameter space. That is, the theorem continues to hold if, for each $(\xi, \eta) \in X \times Y$, either $[\varphi_\xi(\eta, c) > 0, c \in B]$ or $[\varphi_\xi(\eta, c) = 0, c \in B]$.

Condition 6c defines a differentiable likelihood problem. Condition 6d assumes that the Fisher information ι is neither infinitely large nor vanishingly small. If ι is infinite, (8.60) does not effectively bound $\Omega'\Sigma^{-1}\Omega$. If ι is singular, $\Omega'\Sigma^{-1}\Omega$ must be singular. So singularity of ι implies that $\sqrt{N}(b_N - b)$ does not have a limiting distribution. Conversely, if the assumptions of Theorem 2 hold, then ι must be non-singular.

8.4.3 *The moment problem assumption*

Condition 7a assumes that the method of moments estimate being evaluated uses observations of z only as filtered through the transformation $[y(*), x(*)]$. If $g(*, *)$ depends on other features of z, the moment equation $\int g(z, b) dP = 0$ may contain information about b not expressed by the conditional likelihood problem defined in Condition 6. There is then no reason to think that application of the analogy principle to $\int g(z, b) dP = 0$ must yield an estimate with precision bounded by ι^{-1}. After all, ι^{-1} depends on P only through P_{yx}.

Condition 7b strengthens the identification assumption of Condition 7.1a. Condition 7.1a asserts that b solves

$$\int g(y, x, b) dP_{yx} = \int \left[\int g(y, x, b) \varphi_x(y, b) dv_x \right] dP_x = 0 \quad (8.62)$$

Condition 7b states that

$$\int g(y, \xi, b) \varphi_\xi(y, b) dv_\xi = 0, \qquad \xi \in X \quad (8.63)$$

Thus, Condition 7b implies that b solves (8.62) whatever P_x happens to be.

The role of (8.63) in the information bound theorem is that it prevents the moment equation (8.62) from containing information relating b to P_x. If (8.63) were not to hold, then the pair (b, P_x) would have to be such as to make positive values of $\int g(y, \xi, b) \varphi_\xi(y, b) dv_\xi$ balance negative ones in (8.62). So knowledge of P_x would be informative regarding b. If P_x is informative, the information bound of Theorem 3 need not hold. This bound uses the information that b solves a conditional likelihood problem; it does not express any information relating b to P_x.

Condition 7b states not only that (8.63) holds but also that

$$\int g(y, \xi, c) \varphi_\xi(y, c) dv_\xi = 0, \qquad \xi \in X, \ c \in B \quad (8.64)$$

Assume, contrariwise, that Condition 7b does not hold for a given c in B. Then there exists a ξ in X such that $\int g(y, \xi, c) \varphi_\xi(y, c) dv_\xi \neq 0$. But having assumed (8.63), we know that the true parameter value solves $\int g(y, \xi, b) \varphi_\xi(y, b) dv_\xi = 0$. Hence, a failure of (8.64) implies that c is not a feasible parameter value; that is, c is not in B.

Condition 7c is a boundedness assumption. It is used in (8.58) to reverse the order of differentiation and integration, via the bounded convergence theorem.

Note that the proof of Theorem 3 does not use the full force of

Conditions 6 and 7. These conditions assume that certain properties hold on the full parameter space B. The proof remains valid if the relevant properties hold only in a neighborhood of b. We have chosen to impose Conditions 6 and 7 globally rather than locally because the lesser restrictiveness of local assumptions is more apparent than real. We do not know where b is within B. It follows that if we are to apply Theorem 3, Conditions 6 and 7 must hold in a neighborhood of every possible value of b. Hence, these conditions must hold on all of B.

8.4.4 *Application to extremum problem estimates*

Theorem 3 concerns application of the method of moments to a moment equation. Theorem 2′ showed that the limiting distribution of an extremum problem estimate is determined by its associated first-order condition. So Theorem 3 applies to extremum problem estimates. This fact is stated as Theorem 3′.

Theorem 3′
Assume the conditions of Theorem 2′ and Conditions 6 and 7. Then

$$\sqrt{N}(b_N - b) \xrightarrow{L} \mathbf{N}[0, \imath^{-1} + E] \tag{8.65}$$

where E is a positive semidefinite $K \times K$ matrix.   ■

8.4.5 *Attaining the bound*

Theorem 3 does not say whether there exists an asymptotically efficient estimate, that is one whose limiting distribution is $\mathbf{N}(0, \imath^{-1})$. The maximum likelihood method provides such an estimate, provided that the conditional density functions are somewhat smoother than was assumed in Condition 6. Adding Condition 8 suffices. Theorem 4 proves that the maximum likelihood estimate attains the bound.

Condition 8 (Smooth densities)
(a) For $(\xi, \eta) \in X \times Y$, $\varphi_\xi(\eta, *)$ is twice continuously differentiable on B.
(b) For $\xi \in X$, there exists a $D_\xi(*)$ mapping Y into $[0, \infty)$ such that

   (i) The integral $\int D_\xi(y) dv_\xi$ exists and is finite.
   (ii) $|\partial \varphi_\xi(\eta, c)/\partial a| \leqslant D_\xi(\eta), (\eta, c) \in Y \times B$.
   (iii) $|\partial^2 \varphi_\xi(\eta, c)/\partial a \, \partial a'| \leqslant D_\xi(\eta), (\eta, c) \in Y \times B$.

Theorem 4
Assume Condition 6. For $c \in B$, let $X_c \equiv [\xi \in X : \tau_\xi(c) \neq P_y | \xi]$. Assume that $\int_{X_c} dP_x > 0$ for all $c \in B$ such that $c \neq b$. Then b is the unique solution to the moment extremum problem

$$b - \operatorname*{argmax}_{c \in B} \int \log \varphi_{x(z)}[y(z), c] \, dP = 0 \qquad (8.66)$$

Let problem (8.66) satisfy the conditions of Theorem 2'. Let Condition 8 hold. Then

$$\sqrt{N}(b_N - b) \xrightarrow{L} N(0, \iota^{-1}) \quad \blacksquare \qquad (8.67)$$

PROOF That b is the unique solution to (8.66) was shown in Section 5.1. By assumption, the conditions of Theorem 2' hold; so the limiting distribution of $\sqrt{N}(b_N - b)$ is $N(0, \Omega^{-1}\Sigma\Omega'^{-1})$. We need to show that $\Omega^{-1}\Sigma\Omega'^{-1} = \iota^{-1}$.
The first-order condition associated with (8.66) is

$$\int \frac{\partial \log \varphi_{x(z)}[y(z), b]}{\partial a} \, dP = 0 \qquad (8.68)$$

Hence,

$$\Sigma \equiv \int g(z, b)g(z, b)' \, dP$$

$$= \int \frac{\partial \log \varphi_x(y, b)}{\partial a} \frac{\partial \log \varphi_x(y, b)}{\partial a'} \, dP_{yx} = \iota \qquad (8.69)$$

Assume tentatively that Condition 7 holds for

$$g(*, *) \equiv \frac{\partial \log \varphi_{x(*)}[y(*), *]}{\partial a} \qquad (8.70)$$

Then (8.59) implies that

$$\Omega = - \int g(y, x, b) \frac{\partial \log \varphi_x(y, b)}{\partial a'} \, dP_{yx}$$

$$= - \int \frac{\partial \log \varphi_x(y, b)}{\partial a} \frac{\partial \log \varphi_x(y, b)}{\partial a'} \, dP_{yx} = -\iota \qquad (8.71)$$

It follows that $\Omega^{-1}\Sigma\Omega'^{-1} = \iota^{-1}$.

It remains to show that Condition 7 holds. The definition (8.70) shows that part (a) holds. Part (c) is assumed in Condition 8b, as

$$\partial^2 \varphi_\xi(\eta, c)/\partial a \partial a' = \frac{\partial \left[[\partial \log \varphi_\xi(\eta, c)/\partial a] \varphi_\xi(\eta, c) \right]}{\partial a'} \qquad (8.72)$$

To show part (b), observe that

$$\int \varphi_\xi(y, c) \, dv_\xi = 1, \qquad (\xi, c) \in X \times B \qquad (8.73)$$

by Conditions 6a and 6b. Hence,

$$\frac{\partial \int \varphi_\xi(y, c) \, dv_\xi}{\partial a} = 0, \qquad (\xi, c) \in X \times B \qquad (8.74)$$

Conditions 6c and 8b imply, by the bounded convergence theorem, that

$$\frac{\partial \int \varphi_\xi(y, c) \, dv_\xi}{\partial a} = \int \frac{\partial \varphi_\xi(y, c)}{\partial a} dv_\xi$$

$$= \int \frac{\partial \log \varphi_\xi(y, c)}{\partial a} \varphi_\xi(y, c) \, dv_\xi, \qquad (\xi, c) \in X \times B \qquad (8.75)$$

It follows from (8.74) and (8.75) that

$$\int \frac{\partial \log \varphi_\xi(y, c)}{\partial a} \varphi_\xi(y, c) \, dv_\xi = 0, \qquad (\xi, c) \in X \times B \qquad (8.76)$$

So Condition 7b holds.   Q.E.D.

CHAPTER 9

More on limiting distributions

This chapter describes recent contributions that generalize the 'classical' limiting distribution analysis of Chapter 8. Sections 9.1 and 9.2 report work on efficiency bounds. Section 9.3 summarizes findings for non-differentiable moment problems.

9.1 An efficiency bound for moment equation regressions

Chapter 8 presented bounds on the asymptotic precision of estimates of parameters solving two classes of moment problems. Section 8.2 reported an asymptotic minimax bound for differentiable, finite-dimensional moment equations. Section 8.4 proved a version of the information bound for differentiable, finite-dimensional likelihood problems. Recent research provides efficiency bounds for estimates of parameters solving more general versions of these problems. The present section reports an asymptotic minimax bound for differentiable moment equation regressions. Section 9.2 will describe work on semiparametric likelihood problems.

9.1.1 *The estimation problem and the bound*

Let B be a subset of K-dimensional real space, with b interior to B. Let $Z = Y \times X$, where Y and X are subsets of finite-dimensional real spaces. Assume that b solves the collection of moment equations

$$\int g(y, \xi, b)\, dP|\xi = 0, \qquad \xi \in X \tag{9.1}$$

where $g(*, *, *)$ takes values in J-dimensional real space. Assume that the conditional variance matrices

$$\Sigma(\xi) \equiv \int g(y, \xi, b)g(y, \xi, b)'\, dP|\xi, \qquad \xi \in X \tag{9.2}$$

exist and are non-singular. Assume that the $J \times K$ matrices

$$\Omega(\xi) \equiv \int [\partial g(y, \xi, b)/\partial a'] \, dP | \xi, \qquad \xi \in X \qquad (9.3)$$

exist and that the $K \times K$ matrix

$$S \equiv \int \Omega(x)' \Sigma(x)^{-1} \Omega(x) \, dP_x \qquad (9.4)$$

is non-singular.

In this setting, consider the problem of estimating b when it is known that b solves (9.1) and no other information is available. Let $\{b_N\}$ be a sequence of estimates. Chamberlain (1987) finds that, in the asymptotic minimax sense of Hajek, the random variable $\sqrt{N}(b_N - b)$ can be no more concentrated about zero than a random variable distributed $N(0, S^{-1})$. It follows that if $\sqrt{N}(b_N - b)$ has a limiting normal distribution, the variance of this limiting distribution exceeds S^{-1} by a positive semidefinite matrix.

9.1.2 Sketch of the proof

The method of proof is innovative and warrants description. Consider a hypothetical estimation problem in which it is known not only that b solves (9.1) but also that P is multinomial. The support of P is known but the probabilities on these points are not. Chamberlain shows that this hypothetical problem can be represented as a differentiable, finite-dimensional likelihood problem. So classical information bound arguments provide an asymptotic bound for the precision of an estimate of b. It turns out that, asymptotically, $\sqrt{N}(b_N - b)$ can be no more concentrated about zero than a random variable distributed $N(0, S^{-1})$.

Now remove the hypothetical information that P is multinomial. Chamberlain shows that, in all relevant respects, P can be approximated arbitrarily well by a sequence of multinomial measures. In particular, there exists a sequence $Q_m, m = 1, \ldots, \infty$ of multinomial measures on Z which satisfy the conditional moment equations

$$\int g(y, \xi, b) \, dQ_m | \xi = 0, \qquad\qquad \xi \in X, \quad m = 1, \ldots, \infty \qquad (9.5a)$$

$$\int g(y, \xi, b) g(y, \xi, b)' \, dQ_m | \xi = \Sigma(\xi), \qquad \xi \in X, \quad m = 1, \ldots, \infty \qquad (9.5b)$$

$$\int [\partial g(y,\xi,b)/\partial a'] \, dQ_m | \xi = \Omega(\xi), \qquad \xi \in X, \quad m = 1,\ldots,\infty \qquad (9.5c)$$

and which, in a certain sense, converge to P. This implies an asymptotic minimax result.

9.1.3 Application to linear mean regressions

The efficiency bound for differentiable moment equation regressions has many important applications. Perhaps the most prominent is to the problem of estimating the parameter b of a linear mean-regression model. Let $Y = R^1$ and $X = B = R^K$. Let it be known that $E(y|x) = x'b$; no other information is available. So the problem is to estimate b given the knowledge that b solves the collection of conditional moment equations

$$\int (y - \xi'b) \, dP | \xi = 0, \qquad \xi \in X \qquad (9.6)$$

For each $\xi \in X$, let $\sigma^2(\xi)$ denote the unknown variance of $y - \xi'b$. Then

$$\Omega(\xi) = -\xi' \qquad (9.7)$$

$$\Sigma(\xi) = \sigma^2(\xi) \qquad (9.8)$$

and

$$S = \int \sigma^2(x)^{-1} xx' \, dP \qquad (9.9)$$

Observe that if the variance function $\sigma^2(*)$ were known, the weighted least squares estimate

$$B_N \equiv \operatorname*{argmin}_{c \in B} \int \sigma^2(x)^{-1} (y - x'c)^2 \, dP_N \qquad (9.10)$$

would be computable. The limiting distribution for this estimate is $N[0, \{\int \sigma^2(x)^{-1} xx' \, dP\}^{-1}]$. By assumption, $\sigma^2(*)$ is not known so (9.10) is not computable. It is natural to ask whether the variances can be estimated sufficiently well as to yield a feasible estimator that is asymptotically equivalent to (9.10). Subject to regularity conditions, Robinson (1987) answers this question positively.

Note that if $\sigma^2(*)$ really were known, the collection of equations (9.6) would not express all the available information. One would also know that the conditional moment equations

$$\int (y - \xi'b)^2 \, dP|\xi - \sigma^2(\xi) = 0, \qquad \xi \in X \qquad (9.11)$$

hold. Given the knowledge that b solves both (9.6) and (9.11), the efficiency bound is no longer $\mathbf{N}[0, \{\int \sigma^2(x)^{-1}xx' \, dP\}^{-1}]$. So the weighted least squares estimate (9.10) is asymptotically efficient when it is not computable, and inefficient when it is computable.

9.1.4 *Attaining the bound*

An efficiency bound theorem proves that no estimator can outperform the bound; it does not indicate whether the bound is attainable. To show that a bound is sharp, one must find an estimator whose limiting distribution is the bound.

We have reported that Robinson (1987) provides such an estimator for the case of linear mean regression. Earlier, Section 8.2 showed that an estimator proposed by Hansen (1982) attains the bound when the conditioning variable x has one point of support (then $P|\xi = P$). It is easy to see that this estimator remains efficient when x has known finite support. Then the collection of conditional moment equations (9.1) is equivalent to the finite-dimensional moment equation

$$\int 1[x = \xi_i] g(y, x, b) \, dP = 0, \qquad i = 1, \ldots, I \qquad (9.12)$$

where $(\xi_i, i = 1, \ldots, I)$ are the mass points of x. So the results of Chapter 8 apply.

It remains to consider the case in which x may have infinite support. Newey (1986) reports an estimator that attains the bound here. We may therefore conclude that Chamberlain's efficiency bound for differentiable moment equation regressions is sharp.

9.2 Efficiency bounds for semiparametric likelihood problems

An estimation problem is said to be semiparametric if the parameter space has the form $B \times F$, where B is a subset of a finite-dimensional real space and F is a function space. Let $Z = Y \times X$. A parameter $(b, f) \in B \times F$ solves a semiparametric conditional likelihood problem if

$$P_y|\xi = \tau_\xi(b, f), \qquad \xi \in X \qquad (9.13)$$

Here $\tau_\xi(*, *)$ is a given function mapping $B \times F$ into the space of probability measures on Y. The family of measures $[\tau_\xi(c, g), (c, g) \in B \times F]$ are all absolutely continuous with respect to some measure v_ξ on Y.

Recent research has sought to generalize the information bound for finite-dimensional likelihood problems to the much larger class of semiparametric likelihood problems. The discussion that follows emphasizes findings obtained for semiparametric response models. Recall that in a response model, the realization of an observable random variable y is determined by the realization of an observable x, that of an unobservable u, and by the value of a parameter b. Thus (see (6.28)),

$$P_y | \xi = \tau_\xi(b, P_u | \xi), \qquad \xi \in X \qquad (9.14)$$

A response model is semiparametric if b is finite dimensional and the collection of conditional probability measures $f = (P_u | \xi, \xi \in X)$ is known to be in some function space F.

(*Note:* The term 'semiparametric' arises out of the practice of reserving the word 'parametric' for estimation problems involving a finite-dimensional parameter. Problems with a function-valued parameter have long been referred to as 'nonparametric'. So problems having both a parametric and a nonparametric component have come to be called semiparametric. These semantic distinctions are unfortunate: what sense does it make to call a function-valued parameter nonparametric?)

9.2.1 A bound on precision for the finite-dimensional component

Research to date has been concerned primarily with efficient estimation of the finite-dimensional parameter component; the function-valued component is treated as a nuisance parameter. Much of the literature makes use of an idea of Stein (1956).

Stein posed a thought experiment in which the actual estimation problem, having parameter space $B \times F$, is compared with an idealized subproblem in which the parameter space is $B \times F_0$, where $F_0 \subset F$. The actual problem has available less information than does the idealized one. Hence, the actual attainable precision of estimation of b can be no better than the idealized attainable precision.

Suppose that an efficiency bound can be obtained for the idealized subproblem. Such a bound necessarily applies to the actual estimation problem, although it may not be sharp. Stein observed that a bound for the subproblem can be computed whenever F_0 is a differentiable, finite-dimensional family of functions. In this case, the subproblem is a differentiable, finite-dimensional likelihood problem; so the classical information bound holds.

Thus, let

$$F_0 \equiv [f_0(\delta), \delta \in \Gamma] \tag{9.15}$$

where Γ is a subset of a finite-dimensional real space, $f_0(*)$ maps Γ into F, and $f = f_0(\gamma)$ for some γ in Γ. For this subproblem, the Fisher information matrix is

$$I_0 = \begin{bmatrix} A_{bb} & A_{b\gamma} \\ A'_{b\gamma} & A_{\gamma\gamma} \end{bmatrix} \tag{9.16}$$

where

$$A_{bb} \equiv \int \frac{\partial \log \varphi_x[y, (b, \gamma)]}{\partial a} \frac{\partial \log \varphi_x[y, (b, \gamma)]}{\partial a'} dP \tag{9.17a}$$

$$A_{b\gamma} \equiv \int \frac{\partial \log \varphi_x[y, (b, \gamma)]}{\partial a} \frac{\partial \log \varphi_x[y, (b, \gamma)]}{\partial \delta'} dP \tag{9.17b}$$

$$A_{\gamma\gamma} \equiv \int \frac{\partial \log \varphi_x[y, (b, \gamma)]}{\partial \delta} \frac{\partial \log \varphi_x[y, (b, \gamma)]}{\partial \delta'} dP \tag{9.17c}$$

The information bound for estimation of b is the upper left $K \times K$ part of the inverse of I_0, namely $(A_{bb} - A_{b\gamma} A_{\gamma\gamma}^{-1} A'_{b\gamma})^{-1}$. It follows that no actual estimate of b can have better asymptotic precision than this bound. *A fortiori*, no actual estimate can have better asymptotic precision than the infimum of the information bounds for all finite-dimensional subproblems.

Stein did not indicate how the infimum of the bounds for the finite-dimensional subproblems might be computed. Nor did he determine whether this infimum is a sharp bound for the actual semiparametric problem. Nevertheless, his thought experiment has proved useful in analyzing two polar possibilities regarding the limiting behavior of estimates of b. On the one hand, attainable precision in the actual estimation problem may be the same as in the idealized one assuming full knowledge of f. On the other hand, attainable precision in the actual problem may be infinitely worse than in the subproblem assuming f known. Some findings follow.

9.2.2 *Adaptive estimation*

An estimator for b is termed 'adaptive' if its asymptotic precision is the same as the best attainable in the idealized problem in which f is known. Suppose that one wishes to determine whether adaptive estimation of b is possible. Stein's work suggests a necessary condition.

Consider the idealized problem in which f is known. The information bound for estimation of b is A_{bb}^{-1}. Now consider the slightly less idealized subproblem in which Γ is the real line and it is known that f is contained in the space F_0 of (9.15). Here the information bound is $(A_{bb} - A_{b\gamma}A_{\gamma\gamma}^{-1}A_{b\gamma}')^{-1}$. This bound exceeds A_{bb}^{-1} by a non-negative definite matrix. The bounds coincide if and only if

$$A_{b\gamma} = 0 \qquad (9.18)$$

Thus, if F were the one-dimensional space F_0, adaptive estimation of b would be possible if and only if (9.18) holds. In the actual estimation problem, $F_0 \subset F$. Hence (9.18) is not sufficient for existence of an adaptive estimator but remains necessary. Stein concluded that adaptation is impossible if (9.18) fails for any one-dimensional set F_0.

Stein did not indicate how his necessary condition for adaptation might be checked in practice. Bickel (1982) produces a verifiable form of the condition. Bickel's work concerns the class of semiparametric response models in which u is statistically independent of x, P_u is dominated by Lebesgue measure, and convex combinations of feasible densities are themselves feasible. These conditions imply that the space of feasible values for $(P_u | \xi, \xi \in X)$ is representable as a convex space of Lebesgue density functions.

In this setting, Bickel shows that Stein's condition is essentially equivalent to the requirement that b solve each of the misspecified likelihood problems

$$b - \operatorname*{argmax}_{c \in B} \int \log \varphi_x[y,(c,g)]\, \mathrm{d}P = 0, \qquad g \in F \qquad (9.19)$$

In general, b need only solve the correct likelihood problem

$$b - \operatorname*{argmax}_{c \in B} \int \log \varphi_x[y,(c,f)]\, \mathrm{d}P = 0 \qquad (9.20)$$

So the substance of the condition is that b should continue to solve this problem when f is replaced by any g in F.

Bickel finds that his condition is satisfied if the response model has the linear form

$$y - x'b - \alpha - u = 0 \qquad (9.21)$$

where α is a free intercept and F is the space of all densities on U with mean zero. This suggests that b is adaptively estimable. Going on, he proves that an adaptive estimate does exist. Generalizing earlier work of Stone (1975) on adaptive estimation of location parameters, he shows that the following multi-step procedure works:

(i) Estimate (b, α) by least squares or any other method that yields an estimate converging to (b, α) at rate $\sqrt{N}$. Let (b_{0N}, α_{0N}) denote the estimate.

(ii) Compute the residuals $u_{iN} \equiv y_i - x_i'b_{0N} - \alpha_{0N}$, $i = 1, \ldots, N$ and use them to estimate the unknown density function f; Bickel uses a modified kernel estimate.

(iii) Now act as if the estimated density is f and re-estimate (b, α) by a method that would be asymptotically efficient were f known.

Bickel also considers the model (9.21) with F the space of all densities that are symmetric around zero. In this case, not only are the slope parameters b adaptively estimable but also the intercept α.

Manski (1984) extends Bickel's analysis from the linear response model to the class of invertible models. It turns out that b remains adaptively estimable if (9.21) is replaced by the separable model

$$y - h(x, b) - \alpha - u = 0 \qquad (9.22)$$

On the other hand, the necessary condition for adaptation fails to hold in other invertible response models.

9.2.3 Zero Fisher information

Suppose that one wishes to learn whether there exists any estimator of b such that $\sqrt{N}(b_N - b)$ has a limiting distribution. Stein's thought experiment provides a necessary condition.

Let F_j, $j = 1, \ldots, \infty$ be a sequence of increasingly large finite-dimensional subsets of F. Let I_j, $j = 1, \ldots, \infty$ be the corresponding sequence of information matrices. Suppose that $I_j \to 0$ as $j \to \infty$. Then the efficiency bound for the actual estimation problem is zero. It follows, by the Hajek representation theorem, that there exists no estimator such that $\sqrt{N}(b_N - b)$ has a limiting distribution.

Chamberlain (1986) uses this necessary condition to study the attainable precision for estimation of the median-independent binary response model (equation (6.50))

$$y - 1[x'b + u > 0] = 0 \qquad (9.23)$$

For this model,

$$P(y = 1 | \xi) = \int 1[\xi'b + u > 0] \, dP_u | \xi, \qquad \xi \in X \qquad (9.24)$$

The space F of feasible values for $(P_u | \xi, \xi \in X)$ is the set of all collections of probability measures on U that share the same median. Chamberlain finds a particular sequence of finite-dimensional subsets of F for which the information bounds converge to zero.

It is important to understand that a finding of zero Fisher information does not imply either that a parameter is unidentified or that consistent estimation is impossible. In the case of the median-independent binary response model, Manski (1985) proved identification and showed that the estimator given in (6.54) is consistent.

9.2.4 *An information bound for (b, f)*

The work described so far takes the finite-dimensional parameter as the object of interest and the function-valued one as a nuisance parameter. Begun, Hall, Huang, and Wellner (1983) provide an elegant analysis that treats b and f symmetrically.

These authors consider the class of problems in which F is a Hilbert space of functions. The function $\tau(*, *)$ mapping $B \times F$ into the space of probability measures on Z is assumed differentiable in the sense of Hellinger. (See their paper for the definition of Hellinger differentiability.) In this setting, they examine the infinite-dimensional problem of joint estimation of (b, f). Using projection arguments on Hilbert spaces, they obtain infinite-dimensional generalizations of the Fisher information matrix and of the Hajek representation theorem.

The Begun *et al.* analysis has been applied to obtain efficiency bounds for response models in which u is known to be statistically independent of x and P_u is dominated by Lebesgue measure. In particular, Cosslett (1987) computes the information bound for the binary response model (9.23) and finds that it is positive definite. Cosslett also gives the bound for the censored response model of (6.47).

Cosslett's result for the binary response model is not at odds with Chamberlain's finding of zero Fisher information. Whereas Cosslett assumes that u is known to be statistically independent of x, Chamberlain assumes only median independence. Thus, strengthening the available information from median independence to statistical independence appears to increase the attainable rate of convergence for estimation of b.

9.3 Limiting distributions in non-differentiable problems

Chapter 8 showed that, in differentiable moment problems, normalized method of moments estimates have limiting normal distributions. As this book is written, asymptotic distribution theory for non-differentiable problems is developing. Findings for specific problems are accumulating. Moreover, progress is being made towards understanding the critical features of a moment problem that determine the rate of convergence and limiting distribution of a method of moments estimate.

The emerging theory has not yet jelled sufficiently to permit a useful synthesis. We shall suffice with a discussion of two strains of work. One concerns method of moments estimation of quantile regression functions. The other seeks general theorems enabling derivation of limiting distributions for estimates in both differentiable and non-differentiable problems.

9.3.1 *Quantile regressions*

It has long been known that, subject to regularity conditions, the sample median has a limiting normal distribution. Let $y(*)$ map Z into the real line and consider the problem of best prediction of y under absolute loss. The best predictor solves

$$b - \operatorname*{argmin}_{c \in R^1} \int |y(z) - c|\, dP = 0 \qquad (9.25)$$

The method of moments estimate is

$$B_N = \operatorname*{argmin}_{c \in R^1} \int |y(z) - c|\, dP_N \qquad (9.26)$$

The median of P_y solves (9.25); the median of P_{Ny} solves (9.26). The extremum problem (9.25) is non-differentiable; for each ζ in Z, the derivative of $h(\zeta,*) \equiv |y(\zeta) - *|$ fails to exist at $c = y(\zeta)$.

Assume that P_y is dominated by Lebesgue measure μ and has continuous, positive density $\varphi_\mu(*, P_y)$. Then results reported in Section 4.2 imply that the median is the unique solution to (9.25). For $N = 1, \ldots, \infty$, let $b_N \in B_N$. It can be shown that

$$\sqrt{N}(b_N - b) \xrightarrow{L} N\left[0, \frac{1}{4\varphi_\mu(b, P_y)^2} \right] \qquad (9.27)$$

Alternative proofs are given by Cramer (1946, p. 369), Cox and Hinckley (1974, p. 468), and Serfling (1980, p. 252).

This finding for method of moments estimation of a median generalizes to estimation of a linear median regression. Let $x(*)$ map Z into R^K. Let it be known that the median regression of y on x is a linear function $x'b$ for some b in $B = R^K$. Apply the method of moments to the implied extremum problem (see Section 4.3)

$$b - \operatorname*{argmin}_{c \in B} \int |y(z) - x(z)'c| \, dP = 0 \qquad (9.28)$$

The analogy principle yields the least absolute deviations estimate

$$B_N \equiv \operatorname*{argmin}_{c \in B} \int |y(z) - x(z)'c| \, dP_N \qquad (9.29)$$

Problem (9.28) is non-differentiable; for each ζ in Z, the derivative of $|y(\zeta) - x(\zeta)'*|$ fails to exist at c such that $y(\zeta) = x(\zeta)'c$.

Bassett and Koenker (1978) provide conditions under which the least absolute deviations estimate has a limiting normal distribution. They assume that the conditional measures $P_y|\xi$, $\xi \in X$ are a translation family and that the vector x contains a constant component. So we may write

$$y(z) = x(z)'b + u \qquad (9.30)$$

where the random variable u is statistically independent of $x(z)$ and has median zero. They show that if P_u is dominated by Lebesgue measure and has continuous, positive density, then

$$\sqrt{N}(b_N - b) \xrightarrow{L} N\left[0, \frac{1}{4\varphi_\mu(0, P_u)^2} \left(\int xx' \, dP_x \right)^{-1} \right] \qquad (9.31)$$

Observe that the variance matrix in (9.31) differs from that associated with least squares estimation only in the scale factor multiplying the matrix $(\int xx'dP_x)^{-1}$. Here the scale factor is $[1/4\varphi_\mu(0,P_u)^2]$. In least squares it is the variance of P_u. (See Section 8.1.)

Powell (1984) generalizes the Bassett and Koenker result in two respects. Dropping the requirement that the conditional measures $P_y|\xi$, $\xi \in X$ form a translation family, he assumes only that each measure $P_y|\xi$ has median $\xi'b$, is dominated by Lebesgue measure, and has continuous, positive density. He also allows the observations of y to be censored. Instead of observing realizations of (y, x), one observes realizations of $[\max(\delta, y), x]$, where δ is a known constant. Note that setting $\delta = -\infty$ yields the case of no censoring.

Results of Section 6.2 imply that the median regression of $\max(\delta, y)$ on x is $\max(\delta, x'b)$. So b solves the implied extremum problem

$$b - \underset{c \in B}{\operatorname{argmin}} \int |\max[\delta, y(z)] - \max[\delta, x(z)'c]| \, dP = 0 \qquad (9.32)$$

The censored least absolute deviations estimate is

$$B_N \equiv \underset{c \in B}{\operatorname{argmin}} \int |\max[\delta, y(z)] - \max[\delta, x(z)'c]| \, dP_N \qquad (9.33)$$

Powell shows that

$$\sqrt{N}(b_N - b) \xrightarrow{L} \mathbf{N}\left[0, \left[\int \kappa(x) 1[x'b > \delta]xx' \, dP_x \right]^{-1} \right.$$

$$\left. \times \left[\int 1[x'b > \delta]xx'dP_x \right]\left[\int \kappa(x)1[x'b > \delta]xx'dP_x \right]^{-1} \right] \qquad (9.34)$$

where $\kappa(\xi) \equiv 2\varphi_\mu(\xi'b, P_y|\xi)$, $\xi \in X$. In the special case where $P_y|\xi$, $\xi \in X$ are a translation family, $\kappa(\xi) = 2\varphi_\mu(0, P_u)$ for all ξ in X. Then (9.34) reduces to

$$\sqrt{N}(b_N - b) \xrightarrow{L} \mathbf{N}\left[0, \frac{1}{4\varphi_\mu(0, P_u)^2}\left(\int 1[x'b > \delta]xx'dP_x \right)^{-1} \right]$$
$$(9.35)$$

If $P_x(x'b > \delta) = 1$, (9.34) reduces to

$$\sqrt{N}(b_N - b) \xrightarrow{L} \mathbf{N}\left[0, \left[\int \kappa(x)xx' \, dP_x \right]^{-1} \right.$$

$$\left. \times \left[\int xx'dP_x \right]\left[\int \kappa(x)xx'dP_x \right]^{-1} \right] \qquad (9.36)$$

Here, censoring does not affect the limiting distribution.

The above findings for method of moments estimation of linear median regressions extend to linear quantile regressions. See Koenker and Bassett (1978) and Powell (1986) for details. These findings do not generalize to problems in which the random variable y is discrete. Recall the median-independent binary response model. There the median regression of y on x is $1[x'b > 0]$. So b solves the extremum problem

$$b - \operatorname*{argmin}_{c \in B} \int |y(z) - 1[x(z)'c > 0]| \, dP = 0 \qquad (9.37)$$

The least absolute deviations (maximum score) estimate is

$$B_N \equiv \operatorname*{argmin}_{c \in B} \int |y(z) - 1[x(z)'c > 0]| \, dP_N \qquad (9.38)$$

The zero information bound of Chamberlain (1986), noted in Section 9.2, implies that $\sqrt{N}(b_N - b)$ does not have a limiting distribution.

9.3.2 General theorems

Most of the findings to date on limiting distributions in non-differentiable moment problems have been proved using tailor-made approaches, methods that apply only to problems with specific features. One would like to have available general theorems, results that enable derivation of limiting distributions for estimates in broad classes of problems. A step in this direction was made by Huber (1967).

Huber offers an asymptotic normality theorem for method of moments estimates that covers differentiable moment equations and some non-differentiable equations. Huber considers the class of moment equations in which the length K of the parameter vector is the same as the number J of equations. His theorem does not require that the functions $g(\zeta,*)$, $\zeta \in Z$ be differentiable; it suffices that the population moment function $\int g(z, *) \, dP$ be differentiable and satisfy other regularity conditions. The result is as follows.

Theorem (Huber, 1967)
Assume that Conditions 7.1a, 7.7, 8.1, 8.4, and 8.5b hold and that $J = K$. Also assume that the following three conditions hold:

Condition 1 (Differentiability)

The $K \times K$ matrix $\Omega \equiv \partial[\int g(z,b)\mathrm{d}P]/\partial a'$ exists and has rank K.

Condition 2 (Regularity)

There exist $\psi_1, \psi_2, \psi_3, \delta_0 > 0$ such that

(a) $|c - b| \leqslant \delta_0 \Rightarrow \left| \int g(z,c)\mathrm{d}P \right| \geqslant \psi_1 |c - b|, \qquad c \in B$

(b) $|c - b| + \delta \leqslant \delta_0 \Rightarrow \int u(z,c,\delta)\mathrm{d}P \leqslant \psi_2 \delta, \qquad c \in B$

(c) $|c - b| + \delta \leqslant \delta_0 \Rightarrow \int u(z,c,\delta)^2 \,\mathrm{d}P \leqslant \psi_3 \delta, \quad c \in B$

where $u(z,c,\delta) \equiv \sup_{|a-c| \leqslant \delta} |g(z,a) - g(z,c)|$

Condition 3 (Estimate)

b_N, $N = 1, \ldots, \infty$ is a sequence of estimates such that

(a) $|b_N - b| \overset{P}{\longrightarrow} 0$

(b) $\sqrt{N} \int g(z, b_N)\mathrm{d}P_N \overset{P}{\longrightarrow} 0$

Then

$$\sqrt{N}(b_N - b) \overset{L}{\longrightarrow} \mathrm{N}(0, \Omega^{-1}\Sigma\Omega'^{-1}) \quad \blacksquare$$

The conclusion to this theorem is essentially the same as that in Corollary 1 of Theorem 8.2. The two results differ only in the way Ω is defined. Condition 8.2b defined Ω to be $\int [\partial g(z,b)/\partial a'] \mathrm{d}P$. Condition 1 in Huber's theorem concerns $\partial[\int g(z,b)\mathrm{d}P]/\partial a'$. In differentiable problems, these two matrices are equal. In non-differentiable problems, $[\partial g(z,b)/\partial a'] \mathrm{d}P$ is not well defined but $\partial[\int g(z,b)\mathrm{d}P]/\partial a'$ may exist as the integral operator smooths $g(z, *)$.

The primary differences between the assumptions of Theorem 8.2 and those of the present theorem is the restriction imposed on the behavior of the set of functions $g(\zeta, *), \zeta \in Z$ in a neighborhood of b. Whereas Condition 8.2a required that these functions be continuously differentiable, Condition 2 here requires only that they behave regularly when averaged with respect to P.

Huber supposes that the sequence $\{b_N\}$ satisfies Condition 3. Condition 3a requires that the estimate be consistent. Condition 3b requires that as $N \to \infty$, the estimate should, with probability approaching one, come arbitrarily close to solving the sample moment equations, normalized by multiplication by $\sqrt{N}$.

Application of Huber's theorem has been limited by the difficulty of verifying Conditions 1 through 3. The Powell (1984) proof of asymptotic normality for the censored least absolute deviations estimator is among the few econometric applications on record. Recent work aims to develop general theorems with more easily verifiable conditions. In particular, the approach of Pakes and Pollard (1987) appears promising.

References

Amemiya, T. (1974) The non-linear two stage least squares estimator, *Journal of Econometrics*, **2**, 105–110.

Amemiya, T. (1985) *Advanced Econometrics*, Cambridge: Harvard University.

Andrews, D. (1987) Consistency in nonlinear econometric models: A generic uniform law of large numbers, *Econometrica* 155, 6, 1465–1471.

Barlow, R., Bartholomew, D., Bremner, J., and Brunk, H. (1972) *Statistical Inference Under Order Restrictions*, New York: Wiley.

Bassett, G. and Koenker, R. (1978) Asymptotic theory of least absolute error regression, *Journal of the American Statistical Association*, **73**, 618–622.

Begun, J., Hall, W., Huang, W., and Wellner, J, (1983) Information and asymptotic efficiency in parametric–nonparametric models, *Annals of Statistics*, **11**, 432–452.

Bickel, P. (1982) On adaptive estimation, *Annals of Statistics*, **10**, 647–671.

Burguete, J., Gallant, R., and Souza, G. (1982) On unification of the asymptotic theory of nonlinear econometric models, *Econometric Reviews*, **1**, 151–190.

Chamberlain, G. (1986) Asymptotic efficiency in semiparametric models with censoring, *Journal of Econometrics* **32**, 189–218.

Chamberlain, G. (1987) Asymptotic efficiency in estimation with conditional moment restrictions, *Journal of Econometrics*, **34**, 305–334.

Chung, K. (1974) *A Course in Probability Theory*, Orlando: Academic.

Cosslett, S. (1983) Distribution-free maximum likelihood estimator of the binary choice model, *Econometrica*, **51**, 765–782.

Cosslett, S. (1987) Efficiency bounds for distribution-free estimators of the binary choice and the censored regression models, *Econometrica*, **55**, 559–585.

Cox, D. and Hinkley, D. (1974) *Theoretical Statistics*, London: Chapman and Hall.

Cramer, H. (1946) *Mathematical Methods of Statistics*, Princeton: Princeton University.

Ferguson, T. (1967) *Mathematical Statistics: A Decision-Theoretic Approach*, New York: Academic.

Fisher, R. (1925) Theory of statistical estimation, *Proceedings of the Cambridge Philosophical Society*, **22**, 700–725.

Gallant, R. (1987) *Nonlinear Statistical Models*, New York: Wiley.

Goldberger, A. (1968) *Topics in Regression Analysis*, New York: Macmillan.

Hajek, J. (1970) A characterization of limiting distributions of regular estimates, *Z. Wahrscheinlichkeitstheorie verw. Gebiete*, **14**, 323–330.

Hajek, J. (1972) Local asymptotic minimax and admissibility in estimation, *Proceedings of the Sixth Berkeley Symposium on Mathematical Statistics and Probability*, **1**, 175–194, Berkeley: University of California.

Hansen, L. (1982) Large sample properties of generalized method of moments estimators, *Econometrica*, **50**, 1029–1054.

Heckman, J. and Singer, B. (1984) A method for minimizing the impact of distributional assumptions in econometric models for duration data, *Econometrica*, **52**, 271–320.

Huber, P. (1967) The behavior of maximum likelihood estimates under nonstandard conditions, *Proceedings of the Fifth Berkeley Symposium on Mathematical Statistics and Probability*, **1**, 221–233, Berkeley: University of California.

Huber, P. (1981) *Robust Statistics*, New York: Wiley.

Ibragimov, I. and Has'minskii, R. (1981) *Statistical Estimation: Asymptotic Theory*, New York: Springer-Verlag.

Jennrich, R. (1969) Asymptotic properties of non-linear least squares estimators, *Annals of Mathematical Statistics*, **40**, 633–643.

Koenker, R. and Bassett, G. (1978) Regression quantiles, *Econometrica*, **46**, 33–50.

Kolmogorov, A. and Fomin, S. (1970) *Introductory Real Analysis*, Englewood Cliffs: Prentice-Hall.

Lehmann, E. (1983) *Theory of Point Estimation*, New York: Wiley.

Manski, C. (1975) Maximum score estimation of the stochastic utility model of choice, *Journal of Econometrics*, **3**, 205–228.

Manski, C. (1983) Closest empirical distribution estimation, *Econometrica*, **51**, 305–319.

Manski, C. (1984) Adaptive estimation of non-linear regression models, *Econometric Reviews*, **3**, 145–194.

Manski, C. (1985) Semiparametric analysis of discrete response: asymptotic properties of the maximum score estimator, *Journal of Econometrics*, **27**, 313–333.

Newey, W. (1985) Maximum likelihood specification testing and conditional moment tests, *Econometrica*, **53**, 1047–1070.

Newey, W. (1986) Efficient estimation of models with conditional moment restrictions, Department of Economics, Princeton University.

Neyman, J. (1949) Contribution to the theory of the χ^2 test, *Berkeley Symposium on Mathematical Statistics and Probability*, Berkeley: University of California, 239–273.

Pakes, A. and Pollard, D. (1987) The asymptotics of optimization estimators with applications to simulated objective functions, *Econometrica* (forthcoming).

Parr, W. and Schucany, W. (1980) Minimum distance and robust estimation, *Journal of the American Statistical Association*, **75**, 616–624.

Parzen, E. (1962) On estimation of a probability density function and mode, *Annals of Mathematical Statistics*, **33**, 1065–1076.

Pearson, E. (1936) Karl Pearson: an appreciation of some aspects of his life and work, *Biometrika*, **28**, 193–257.

Pearson, K. (1894) Contributions to the mathematical theory of evolution, *Philosophical Transactions of the Royal Society of London*, A, **185**, 71–78.

Pollard, D. (1984) *Convergence of Stochastic Processes*, New York: Springer-Verlag.

Powell, J. (1984) Least absolute deviations estimation for the censored regression model, *Journal of Econometrics*, **25**, 303–325.

Powell, J. (1986) Censored regression quantiles, *Journal of Econometrics*, **32**, 143–155.

Prakasa Rao, B. L. S. (1983) *Nonparametric Functional Estimation*, Orlando: Academic.

Rao, C. R. (1973) *Linear Statistical Inference and Its Applications*, New York: Wiley.

Reiersol, O. (1941) Confluence analysis by means of lag moments and other methods of confluence analysis, *Econometrica*, **9**, 1–24.

Reiersol, O. (1945) Confluence analysis by means of instrumental as of variables, *Arkiv Fur Matematik, Astronomi Och Fysik*, **32A**, no. 4, 1–119.

Robertson, T. and Wright, F. (1975) Consistency in generalized isotonic regression, *Annals of Statistics*, **3**, 350–362.

Robinson, P. (1987) Asymptotically efficient estimation in the presence of heteroskedasticity of unknown form, *Econometrica* (forthcoming).

Rockafellar, R. T. (1970) *Convex Analysis*, Princeton: Princeton University.

Rosenblatt (1956) Remarks on some nonparametric estimates of a density function, *Annals of Mathematical Statistics*, **27**, 832–837.

Rust J. (1986) The asymptotic distribution of randomly para-meterized elements of separable Banach spaces, *Social Systems Research Institute Paper 8634*, Department of Economics, University of Wisconsin-Madison.

Sahler, W. (1970) Estimation by minimum discrepancy methods, *Metrika*, **16**, 85–106.

Sargan, J. (1958) The estimation of economic relationships using instrumental variables, *Econometrica*, **26**, 393–415.

Serfling, R. (1980) *Approximation Theorems of Mathematical Statistics*, New York: Wiley.

Silverman, B. (1986) *Density Estimation*, London: Chapman and Hall.

Stein, C. (1956) Efficient nonparametric testing and estimation, *Proceedings of the Third Berkeley Symposium on Mathematical Statistics and Probability*, **1**, 187–195, Berkeley: University of California.

Stone, C. (1975) Adaptive maximum likelihood estimators of a location parameter, *Annals of Statistics*, **3**, 267–284.

Stone, C. (1977) Consistent nonparametric regression, *Annals of Statistics*, **5**, 595–645.

Tauchen, G. (1985) Diagnostic testing and evaluation of maximum likelihood models, *Journal of Econometrics*, **30**, 415–443.

Von Mises, R. (1947) On the asymptotic distribution of differentiable statistical functions, *Annals of Mathematical Statistics*, **18**, 309–348.

Wolfowitz, J. (1953) Estimation by the minimum distance method, *Annals of the Institute of Statistics and Mathematics*, **5**, 9–23.

Wolfowitz, J. (1957) The minimum distance method, *Annals of Mathematical Statistics*, **28**, 75–88.

Wright, S. (1928) Appendix B to Wright, P. *The Tariff on Animal and Vegetable Oils*, New York: Macmillan.

Index